MY

BOYFRIEND

WROTE

A BOOK

ABOUT

ME

MY BOYFRIEND

WROTE A BOOK

ABOUT ME

AND OTHER STORIES I SHOULDN'T SHARE WITH ACQUAINTANCES, COWORKERS, TAXI DRIVERS, ASSISTANTS, JOB INTERVIEWERS, BIKINI WAXERS, AND EX/CURRENT/FUTURE BOYFRIENDS BUT HAVE

Hilary Winston

STERLING
New York

STERLING
New York

An Imprint of Sterling Publishing
387 Park Avenue South
New York, NY 10016

STERLING and the distinctive Sterling logo are registered trademarks of
Sterling Publishing Co., Inc.

2 4 6 8 10 9 7 5 3 1

Distributed in Canada by Sterling Publishing
c/o Canadian Manda Group, 165 Dufferin Street
Toronto, Ontario, Canada M6K 3H6
Distributed in the United Kingdom by GMC Distribution Services
Castle Place, 166 High Street, Lewes, East Sussex, England BN7 1XU
Distributed in Australia by Capricorn Link (Australia) Pty. Ltd.
P.O. Box 704, Windsor, NSW 2756, Australia

Manufactured in the United States of America

Sterling ISBN 978-1-4027-7979-4

For information about custom editions, special sales, premium and
corporate purchases, please contact Sterling Special Sales
Department at 800-805-5489 or specialsales@sterlingpublishing.com.

This book is dedicated to my favorite cats (you know who you are) and anyone who has ever had their heart broken. And dreamed of getting just the tiniest slice of revenge. And didn't do it because they were worried they'd look crazy. I'm taking this bullet for you. You're welcome.

CONTENTS

Part 4: No More Baths (Well, Maybe a Few More)

This section will tell the stories from my acting out phase.
This will be the section that will most embarrass my family
members and possibly even my friends and neighbors.

Part 5: Terrible, Horrible, No Good, Very Bad Things, and One Crazy-ass Mailman

The truth hurts and these essays are achingly true. They include my mother's breast cancer, me putting my cat into a diabetic coma on my birthday (sorry, Emmett), and other things that attract male companions.

Part 6: Where Do Broken Vaginas Go? Do They Find Their Way Home?

Every good book or fight has a wrap up. This chapter is about how I mended my heart and broke my vagina, literally.

A NOTE TO THE READER

This book is painfully true. The stories are told the way I remember them happening and reflect my personal opinion on people, events, and ultimately the truth. Some details have been changed to protect the innocent/guilty. But the only person I really intended to make fun of at all in this book is myself and maybe my diabetic cat. If you are one of the guys I dated and are written about in here, I'm sorry. But we had fun . . . yes? Maybe. And c'mon, *you* probably broke up with me.

PREFACE

A little background before we go any further together, I *am* a lady.

I was born in Los Angeles, California, to a government lawyer and a swimwear designer. I have a therapist sister, Christine, who is four years older and according to my mother, much, much smarter than me. She took an IQ test in elementary school that revealed she was a genius. I was given no such test but I guess my parents figured the chances of birthing two geniuses were slim. That's how I became the dumber sister. We moved to Corpus Christi, Texas, in 1980 so my Dad could work in the family auto parts business and I could develop a slight Texan accent.

After paying four years tuition at The George Washington University (go Colonials), my parents encouraged/begged/blackmailed me to become a lawyer and make all their dreams come true. This didn't come out of nowhere, I had encouraged it. I went to college hoping to become the first female Republican President, even skipped my junior year of high school to get a jump on the other aspiring lady elephants. Upon arriving in Washington, D.C., I joined the Collegiate Conservatives. After an awkward BBQ with a bunch of pale Republicans in khaki shorts quoting Rush Limbaugh, I almost immediately lost faith in my conservative roots, and went 180 degrees in the other direction. I ended up an intern in the West Wing of the

White House for Bill Clinton, just in time for that job description to become a national punch line.

To add to my further moral decline, I joined our college comedy group, Recess. We performed improv and sketch like it was our job and in writing those sketches my love for comedy was born. It's like a ghost. Once you see it, you can't deny its existence. Once I found comedy, I couldn't deny it was what I wanted to do. By the time I graduated college with a degree in International Affairs, and affairs with guys who didn't really like me back, I'd swung completely to the left and was working as an assistant at NPR. My parents might refer to this time as "the beginning of the end." It's also when I got cats.

When I told my parents I wanted to be a writer, they said "no." They were my primary investors after all. I don't think they wanted to squash my dreams. I just don't think they pictured their little pumpkin writing fart and poo jokes for a living. At least I was a lawyer on my high school Mock Trial team that won state. I did make the Dallas newspaper, so they've got that.

I know my career choice disappointed my parents even though for all intents and purposes, I've "made it." I've been writing television sitcoms professionally (kind of an oxymoron) for almost eight years. I know my parents are proud of me although sometimes they deflect having to admit this by saying, "You must be so proud of yourself." Point being, they have come to appreciate my job on some level but I'm about to disappoint them again by doing something very un-Southern: air my dirty laundry. I'm thirty-four years old and I have stories I feel the need to tell, including one about the death of a relationship and its resurrection in the "New Fiction" section at Barnes & Noble. In fact, that story is the inspiration for telling them all.

My stories aren't Lifetime Movie Network material. I was not kidnapped and fed ground meat as a child. I did not overcome a terrible illness and go on to find a cure for Restless Leg Syndrome in a dwindling rainforest. I did not adopt a deaf child (though I almost adopted a blind kitten . . . almost, too needy). And I did not donate my eggs or re-virginize myself in front of Congress.

But things happen. Life happens. Over the course of a few years, I fell in love. I fell out of love. My sex robot obsessed significant other decided to cryogenically freeze himself. My mom got cancer and bragged about the weight she lost. My cat got diabetes. I gave an accidental hand job. I broke my vagina, literally. I bought a house. I had a questionable poo. I got all my private's hair waxed off. I ate Tylenol PM and Lean Cuisine for dinner. And just when I thought my Job-like phase was coming to an end, my ex-boyfriend wrote a book about me.

My ex-boyfriend didn't get our story right. And I've had quite a few interesting stories since then. So what's a good Texas girl turned comedy writer to do, but write a tell-all book of essays to set the record straight for all my exes. So, here you go: the "best of/worst of" version of my life.

PART 1

MY
BOYFRIEND
WROTE
A BOOK
ABOUT ME

I AM THE FAT-ASSED GIRLFRIEND

It's a weekday in sunny Los Angeles and I want to rip his dick off. I'm in the Barnes & Noble at The Grove, an outdoor shopping center in the middle of Hollywood that has a large, well-groomed, unnatural park at the heart of it with a small imitation Bellagio fountain. "Imitation" being used extremely loosely. At Christmastime it "snows" bubbles, to the delight of L.A. shoppers hungry for changing seasons. People bring their families and strollers on the weekends. The masterminds behind The Grove, which is largely shaped like a maze or trap with very few exits, try to make you feel like you're somewhere special, an enclave in the bustling sea of urban disappointment, but no matter what it snows, it's just a damn mall.

It's a beautiful day. It's the kind of day a kid paints with their watercolors—big yellow sun, fluffy white clouds, and an unrealistic bright blue sky. There aren't many windows in the bookstore. It's the middle of the afternoon in the middle of the week and the bookstore is packed. I don't know why it's always so packed. It's just a bookstore. Libraries aren't this packed and they have the same thing. For free! There are so many tourists, which blows my mind. If you are a tourist in L.A. why are you at Barnes & Noble? I'm sure it's the same as every other Barnes & Noble.

For whatever reason, people are here strolling down the aisles judging the books by their covers. And the same people judging the books are also judging the people hunched over reading those books, spilling coffee and biscotti crumbs all over *The Lovely Bones* which they don't intend to purchase but will enjoy for now. It's calm and everyone is library quiet. But I don't want to be quiet. I want to scream and cry and stab my fucking heart out with their chocolate-dipped biscotti but that's not okay to do in the middle of Barnes & Noble on a weekday. Possibly a weekend when there is more noise, but not now, not in a half-full, three-tiered store with amazing acoustics. I'll be thrown out; I'll be dragged out. I'll fight and yell and bite the security guard because I don't feel like I can be anything but insane at this moment. And it's all my fault.

I wasn't even near it. I was in the travel section buying books on Turkey, where I'm going with my platonic best friend Len. We're going to share a bed and incredible life experiences because I have a *life*. I've moved on. I know things about wine, red AND white. I buy *The Economist* when I fly and sometimes even read it. I have dinner parties or at least have had *one*. And despite all that, it pulls me in, like a conversation about ex-girlfriends. You know it isn't going to be good but you just can't resist. I can't see anything else in the store. In this store full of so many books, so many better reviewed books, I can only see his. *His* name. The name I used to scribble on yellow legal pads, adding Mrs. to the front of it like a fourth-grade girl on the back of a school bus. The name I thought would be on my wedding invitations and monogrammed stationary, towels, and party napkins. The name I thought I would give to my kids. But instead, his name is on this book and on someone else's legal pad. And I can't breathe.

———

Kyle and I met at an Ivy League Drinks Mixer at the Liquid Kitty, a dark martini bar, in 2000. Martinis and cigars were the in things at the moment, but I didn't partake in either. I was twenty-three years old, and didn't have much in the way of long-term relationship experience or real life experience.

Neither of us went to Ivy League schools but some of our friends did. I always wanted to date an Ivy League guy, maybe because I had a complex about not attending one. I would've tried harder to get in but I didn't realize what a big deal it was.

A jerk guy (Dartmouth) bumped into me. Classic move. I was avoiding talking to the jerk guy (who had a lot of questions but wasn't interested in the answers) and ended up talking to his friend, Kyle. Kyle was on the short side and had fine blonde hair that struggled to cover his forehead, blue eyes, freckles, and pale skin. You could tell he worked out, maybe too much for my taste. I found out we were both from Texas. I smiled. He smiled. I wore my hair pulled tightly back into a librarian bun, a wreck of blonde highlights at the time and pants I looked fat in. Girls with sizeable behinds should not wear Capri pants no matter how fashionable they are. This is a trap I have fallen into more than once. I am publicly apologizing now.

I wrote my number down for Kyle on my boss's business card (I was an assistant to a TV producer and didn't even have my own cards) and wrote underneath it "Texan Girl." In my head I guess I was worried if he got another girl's phone number he would get us confused. That's before I really knew Kyle. He wasn't one to hit on girls. He's self-admittedly scared of girls. "We" happened by accident. I know he still has this "Texan Girl" card. And though California is now our home we're both still Texans at heart. I like dating Texans. Texans have this weird love of the state but since we made the choice to leave it, we know it's not perfect. Kyle called me a few days after we met. He sounded like he was on the verge of laughing.

"Hey, this is Kyle. We met at the Liquid Kitty."

I was excited and covered it with the driest tone I could muster, "I remember." My tone clearly caused Kyle to lose whatever confidence he had going into the call, "So, do you want to get a drink sometime?"

I gasped audibly then said, "What? I'm not good enough for dinner?"

Oh, the confidence of youth. Kyle picked me up at my shitty dilapidated apartment which was crammed at the bottom of the Hollywood Hills for our first date. The apartment complex had been a crack house seemingly months before I moved in. My front door had crowbar marks and the inside had roaches. I didn't pick it, one of my gay ex-boyfriends did.

The first week I moved in I was at the manager's apartment giving him a check when another tenant stormed in yelling in very formal English, enunciating every word clearly, something very close to the following, "Sir, I think you should know that I have just telephoned the police. Because my roommate has locked himself in the bathroom with a bunch of *my* cocaine and a hooker . . . again."

My upstairs neighbor was a speed freak who used to always borrow toilet paper from me at ridiculous hours and repaid me in donuts. It was just like the ad said, "Charming 1 Br in Hllwd Hlls with view." The view was of a neon motel sign (The Falcon) unless you stood on the bed and then you could see the Hollywood Hills. The previous owner had a dog and it smelled like dog pee. The manager's response to my complaint was, "Wait. You know what it really smells like? That stuff you clean dog pee with." Charming was right.

At that time the neighborhood was too dangerous to walk in, but sometimes I would drive to 7-11, not far from "Pla-boy Liquor" another choice spot where I once saw two homeless people huddled over a box next to the parking lot. Upon closer inspection of what they were hunched over, I saw that it was a giant sheet cake that said, "Congratulations on your 100th episode." Welcome to Hollywood. Irony like this was as common as lavandarias. A local stop for actors seeking headshots was next to the anonymous needle exchange. But after a few years, posh nightclubs replaced strip clubs, the Kodak Theatre (where the Oscars are held) replaced "3 for $10" T-shirt shops, and Starbuck's replaced donut/Chinese food shops. And quickly the neighborhood lost all its "charm."

Kyle ventured into my sub-par neighborhood from his Westside one. Westside living was a little easier. The biggest problem was street cleaning. Kyle arrived for our first date on time but waited at the wrong side of my building for 15 minutes. It was a side door, not the front entrance. I was annoyed he was late. He was annoyed I was late. It was our first but certainly not our last fight. He made a joke about me living on the corner of Dix and Wilcox streets. I was too nervous and too much of a lady then to get it.

Kyle had a black embroidered keychain that said "Jesus 2000." I was worried he might be too Christian for me. Little did I know that he would later write a book describing the details of famous "cunt's" vaginas. Precious.

Kyle took me to an old style Italian place named Micheli's with red-and-white-checked plastic tablecloths and dusty papier-mâché vegetables. He confessed later it was the only restaurant he really knew in town that wasn't a nationwide chain. The kind of place only two struggling Hollywood assistants would describe as "classy." Kyle was just out of film school and in between jobs, the kind of guy who populated cafes and bookstores at one o'clock on a Tuesday.

Kyle wore the shirt I would later find out was his "fancy shirt," gray, synthetic, and shiny. I wore my "cool" outfit, sleeveless lime green Spandex top, grey stretch pants, and red platform sandals. It was still the early nineties in my closet. Since I was fairly new to L.A., I hadn't realized I was "fat" yet. I hit the white crusty warm bread the second it landed at our small, cramped table. Chianti is what I ordered to drink because it was the only wine I'd really ever had. Kyle and I talked non-stop the whole dinner. We talked about writing and what makes something funny and how hard it is to actually "make it." We talked about why most women aren't funny (society raises the fart jokes out of women). He told me I was the funniest woman he'd ever met. We talked about how hard it was going to be to become writers and though we didn't say it, you could tell we were both nervous about our chances.

We compared notes on growing up in Texas. I told him I felt like an expatriate having moved away. We both had conservative parents who would rather we be lawyers than pursue our dreams. I don't remember what I ordered because it didn't matter. Nothing mattered but us. I was bothered by the waiter coming by to ask if we wanted to order, more water, dessert, the check. All I wanted to do was talk to Kyle. My chest was flushed, a super secret and totally public sign of my real interest in someone. When we were finishing, a guy walked out in a full suit of squeaky armor and proposed to the girl sitting next to us. If it had been a scene in a movie you wouldn't have believed it. You would think, "nobody actually does that." The lucky girl was crying so hard you could barely hear her squeak out a yes. But she did. The room filled with applause and toasts and hopes for their future.

I said to Kyle half-joking, "That's weird that we're on our first date. And one first date eventually leads to that."

I smiled. He shit his pants. I thought, *Please let this be the one.* He thought, *Could her ass possibly be that fat?*—or so I found out later.

After dinner I invited him up to my apartment, which he thought meant fooling around, and I thought meant more conversation about comedy, writing, life, school, traffic, and why I had two cats and several gay ex-boyfriends. At the end of the night, he wanted to kiss me but my cat, Emmett, cockblocked him. Owning two cats in general is a cockblock. It took a long time for Kyle to kiss me.

The day after my first date with Kyle, I went to my trendy West Hollywood gym, Crunch, which is located in a shopping center with an indie movie theatre and a store that seemed to only sell gay men's active wear. I saw Kyle and his friend, Benny (who I didn't know at the time). I looked like crap; I was wearing too-small gym shorts and a sweaty T-shirt that said "Las Vegas 2000" with an alien on it. So I did what any brave, self-respecting lady would do. I hid.

Later, I found out that Kyle was having lunch at California Pizza Kitchen (one of Kyle's few acceptable eating establishments) with Benny to discuss our first date. Benny relayed Kyle's side of the conversation to me one night after a few drinks:

> "I went out with this really cool girl last night,
> but she has the biggest ass I have ever seen."

Benny wasn't trying to hurt me. I think he was trying to be amusing but he could have left out the word "ever." He could have said, "The biggest ass I've seen in a long time."

When Kyle and I first started dating we went to the indie movie theatre in that mall. We saw a movie called *Jesus' Son* and as I came up the escalator I was shocked to find Kyle in ice colored, acid washed jeans, which I later found out had a shorts counterpart. A grown man in acid washed jean shorts. It was almost a deal-breaker. Just like my giant ass.

After our fourth date at a campy Mexican restaurant with flaming margaritas and waiters desperate to turn tables, we came back to my place and made casual conversation on my beige IKEA as-is couch and I said, "So, are you ever going to kiss me or what?"

Then he leaned in and did it. As a rule, I hate first kisses. They are awkward and make me sweat in weird places. But this was the worst first kiss ever. My lips were pressed tightly together like my mother was trying to feed me Robitussin, which is a weird thing to think when you are getting kissed. My low self-esteem felt like he was just doing it because I asked. Luckily it got better.

And that was it. After a few more weeks of dating we were inseparable. Kyle was my first real boyfriend. The first guy to take me home to meet his parents. The first guy I had sex with a significant number of times. The first guy to care whether or not I finished during sex. The first guy to take care of me when I got the stomach flu (over New Year's 2001, lost five pounds!). The first guy to buy me a birthday cake. The first guy to leave me a note on my bed telling me he couldn't wait to see me again so I would find it when I came home from work. The first guy to find toilet paper in my butt. The first guy who ever said he loved me.

It's sweet, right? He played baseball; I took improv classes at the Groundlings comedy theatre. He drank beer; I drank Diet Coke. He had OCD; I was messy. He had a perfect hairless body; I had never been waxed. We took a bath together every morning and every night. When we first started dating, he lived in a dark dingy condo from the '70s that had this tiny weird tub in the bathroom. If you pulled a computer keyboard key out and turned it upside down that was its shape. We sat in it Indian style. Sometimes we turned off the lights and lit candles. It was always where serious conversations took place, which was good. It's hard to get really angry at someone when you're naked and squeezed into a tiny weird tub. Kyle and I ate at the Olive Garden every Sunday night. The waiters knew our order by heart (salad and breadsticks as a meal with dipping sauce, half marinara, half alfredo, for me. Chicken Parm for him). We wrote script after script, chased opportunity after opportunity, always wondering if we could possibly be the ones who actually made it in Hollywood. And it turns out we were. It just didn't happen when we were together.

———————

His book is stacked high in three different colors (red, blue, black). It has no cover art, just the basic title and a story inside that is anything but average to me. The title font is plain and simple and if I didn't know the name printed at the bottom in the same plain and simple font I would be drawn to it. But I am repelled by this book. I don't want to read this book. But, here it is. And here I am . . . sweating. I have dry mouth. I am shaking. I am going to throw up.

The first line of the first page I open to says something about his fat-assed girlfriend taking Groundlings improv classes. I die. Right there I die. I took Groundlings improv classes. I have a fat ass. I was his girlfriend. But this book is in the fiction section. This is supposed to be fucking FICTION. Where is the fiction? I frantically flip through the pages, words, people, places, memories, flashing through my head. Remember the guy proposing to his girlfriend in a suit of armor? In there! And the main character is in a long-term relationship with his fat-assed girlfriend. Remember my fat ass?! And they live by UCLA. We lived by UCLA! I hadn't mentioned that yet, but we did.

———————

I wanted to move in with Kyle after a year of dating. For me it was about getting to that next level with someone. It was about not losing him. He resisted. He was worried we would just become roommates. I finally stopped bringing it up. Then one day, he was ready.

We took the first place we saw. It was in Westwood, near UCLA, just a few blocks from his old apartment. I wanted to live farther east but this was my sacrifice. The place was gorgeous. Looked like an English Manor. Two stories. Two bedrooms. Two parking spots. Two bathrooms. Two entrances. Two of us. One giant bathtub. The apartment complex was built in the '30s and our place still had some of the original furniture. Allegedly two Oscar winners had once lived there but their names had long since been forgotten. We took this as a sign. We signed a two-year lease. I negotiated the lease and one of the ways I got them to drop the price was to say we were saving to get married which I thought we were. It turns out I was saving for a house I would buy alone.

———————————

I skim through his book, my heart racing, cheeks flushed. This book is our life. Our friends, our family, our sex. This book is dripping with our sex. The moments we've talked about over and over. The "You do this"es (you sleep at my baseball games) and "You do that"s (you never stop talking about robots) that you laugh about until you have a fight and use them as ammunition. Each page is a betrayal; each page rips a piece of clothing off of me until I am standing naked before middle-age tourists in the Barnes & Noble. There are so many copies of this book, and I want to hide it like a dirty sex tape. We actually made a sex tape once, handheld. And when we watched it back all Kyle said was, "I look fat." Kyle! Everyone looks fat in 69. 69 with the character of "me" is all over this book. I wonder what his parents are going to think?!

I miss his folks. Every time I fly through DFW, I think of them and his sister. His mother's chocolate cinnamon cake and easy laugh, his dad's obsession with college football, his sister, who I never saw out of a sweatshirt, and her amazing sketches. Their teacup Chihuahua, Corky, whose poop looked like Tootsie Rolls. His mom and sister are now my Facebook friends. We'll see what happens when they read this.

At Kyle's sister's wedding, I was insanely jealous. Jealous that two people were so sure of what they wanted. She was five years younger and had met her husband after I met Kyle. I was in charge of the guest book, which apparently nobody signed and I think the family is still sore over it. Kyle told me the night of their traditional black and white, formal, red rose fantasy wedding that he could never see himself doing it, getting married, even in the distant future. I was devastated. I cried in the hallway outside their honeymoon suite. Most people catch romance at a wedding, not repulsion.

Kyle didn't want marriage, but there was some part of him that wanted kids, who he could shape and mold. That was my "in," I thought. We took many baths and talked many times about what we would name our kids. I liked Clementine or Winston. He liked Robot or Dead. I told him "Robot" sounded too much like "Robert" and that everyone would just call the kid "Robert." I thought I had brilliantly won this argument until he came up with "Dead." He thought it would be hilarious to have a little tiny baby in a stroller and when people would ask, "Oh, who's this cute little guy?" Kyle could say, "Dead." The joy he saw in this was the uncomfortable reaction people would have. Uncomfortable reactions are one of Kyle's favorite things.

While we were dating, we went on trips separately that made us miss each other. We went on trips together that made us miss our home. We made our house a home. A cocktail of the laundry he'd never put away and my Gap sale clothes that couldn't fit in the closet. My cats and his action figures. His sci-fi books and my self-help ones. We ate salad and breadsticks as a meal, we went to the gym together; we saved our money for things that would be left out on the curb for families crammed in rundown mini-vans to take in the night. We begged, we hoped, we prayed (non-religiously) for writing jobs that would make us call our parents/exes/popular kids in high school and say, "I told you so."

We were more than this paperback in three different colors stacked high on a sale table, more than fodder for the mid-afternoon looky-loos. I was destroyed. This was it. And he didn't even have the nerve to do it in non-fiction.

We had dinner six months before the book was published, the first time since we'd broken up, at an Italian place called Dominic's. It was the upscale version of the place we went to on our first date. I asked him to go; he confessed he thought maybe I'd gotten engaged and wanted to tell him. I was so flattered he would think that, but of course I was at the messy end of a relationship with someone terrible for me and he was at the beginning of one with someone he thought was great. I asked who was prettier, his new girlfriend or me. As I heard the words come out of my mouth I was embarrassed for myself. The answer didn't much matter[1] because he was taking baths with her. She was mad we were having dinner. I wished the guy I was dating cared if I screwed somebody else.

Over spaghetti and crusty white bread (just like our first date), Kyle told me he sold a book. I was happy and sad and jealous and worried he made more money than me.

I said with a forced smile, "That's awesome." Kyle casually responded, "Yeah. It's pretty cool. It's what I've always wanted."

Our words were generic but had weight. I'd felt like this before. When I was still living in D.C., I ran into an ex-boyfriend from college on the subway. We exchanged hellos and small talk. I hadn't seen him since he tore my heart out with his dirty Phish-head fingernails. As we stood there, waiting anxiously for our stop, we talked about the weather. The weather! I wanted to scream at the top of my lungs for all the commuters to hear, "You've seen me naked. You asshole! I don't care what you have to say about the goddamn fucking rain!"

This dinner situation with Kyle reminded me of that day. The last time I saw him, I wanted to spit in his face and now we were pleasantly deciding whether we should order sparkling or still water. We looked like two people just comfortably having dinner and catching

---

[1] He said me.

up, when really there was a storm of emotion inside of me. Kyle tells me his book comes out in the spring. He tells me nothing else about it. No heads up. No "Just so you know this is loosely based on our life together and will destroy you" kind of a warning.

If he had told me then, it still would have hurt. But at least I would have known. I could have asked questions. "How could you do this to me? Why was this necessary? Is there a passage wherein you describe my vagina in excessive detail?" Stuff like that. At least I wouldn't be standing here alone in this bookstore, holding this novel like a tiny wash cloth in front of my naked body not knowing which private part to cover. How dare he call this fiction! I want to scream in his freckled face. We broke up because Kyle decided he didn't want to get married and have kids, not because we didn't love each other, right? Or did I fall for a "this will make her feel better" break up lie? I want to ask him what the truth really is. I want to ask him: "Are you not man enough for non-fiction? Why was I not enough for you? Why did you feel you had to break up with me at the lowest point of my life? Why won't we ever be over each other? Why were you too much of a pussy to marry me? I get the sense from your book that my ass was somewhat larger than what you're used to, care to comment?" This is insulting. This is heartbreaking. This is passive aggressive. This is torture. I would have preferred a straight out fight to this "fiction." But this is what I got.

Kyle started writing his book the week after we broke up. And at the hands of his unnamed narrator, our story ended and my book of stories began, which, by the way, you will find in the "non-fiction" section because it will include more than just thinly veiled truths. It will include fully realized truths like the fact that my ex has white nut hairs. Sue me, "Kyle." You know it's true.

PART 2

THE

FOUNDATION

IS

CRACKED

IT ALL STARTED
WITH A GARBAGE PAIL KID

At the age of thirty a well-meaning guy would put his pinky in my butt but long before that, my love life began innocently enough. The start of my romantic existence came in a crisp white business envelope in neatly written print containing a love letter on an index card. It was one of the first pieces of mail that I'd ever received. I was in ponytails and the third grade. That year's school picture was one of my favorites—lopsided smirk, smart pink Polo shirt dress with a kelly green grosgrain ribbon belt.

I had a confidence I would lose as soon as fourth grade rounded the corner with a nude colored training bra in its hand.

I went upstairs to my bedroom after taking the letter, embarrassed, out of my mother's judgmental hand. Other things I have taken from my mother's judgmental hand include money, *Flowers in the Attic*, a brochure from Columbia

University in New York City(?!), the phone with an older college boy on the end of it, and the first birth control prescription I had filled at seventeen (for "cramps"). Alone, I carefully opened the envelope, not tearing it even the tiniest bit. Even though I didn't know the contents, I knew it was special. The well-thought out love communication with impressive penmanship came from the small freckled hand of school-mate Nathan Doreen. Postmarked February 21, 1986. Nathan was a skinny kid, almost to the point of emaciated. I think he ate but just couldn't keep any weight on. He'd have an old man belt holding up his pants or he wore acid-washed Oshkosh B'Gosh elastic waistband jeans. A look not even a third-grader can really feel good about, but you couldn't blame him. He didn't buy his own clothes. He was redheaded and pale faced with a bowl cut that was shockingly close to Dorothy Hamill's. He was also smart and quiet and the kind of kid who would rather be unpopular than make fun of someone else.

The index card he sent was crisp and folded. A crease that had been painstakingly made, while I'm sure Nathan questioned his entire plan and his heart beat out of his chest like a cartoon. But man, was he courageous. At that age, there were so many steps to sending a letter on your own. He would have had to explain himself at a number of parental checkpoints. He had to ask for an envelope and a stamp and the Doreen family's return address label with the American flag on it, which he corrected to say just Nathan Doreen in case by mistake I thought the love letter was from his dad. But he had a drive that made him fearless.

At that age, roughly eight, his intention was pure. He didn't know why, but he liked a girl and he felt compelled to do something about it. That's how it all starts. And as that drive grows, it's the gateway to real emotion. Emotion that moves mountains and starts wars and makes mix tapes and buys airbrushed lovers' T-shirts at the beach and writes horrible songs with simple guitar chords. But it's the gateway to love and passion and rage and fear and jealousy and envy and self-hatred. And the beauty of Nathan's love note is that the igniting of this drive is frozen in time, isolated in a few belabored sentences in number two pencil and for that reason profoundly perfect. I still have it:

Dear Hilary,

Do you like me? I like you! Please send me a picture of you.

> Love,
> Nathan D.

PS: I think your [sic] pretty!

Nathan also included a "Babbling Brooke" Garbage Pail Kid trading card as a gift. She was a pudgy brunette talking on the phone, covered in peanut butter and jelly from her Wonder Bread sandwich. These cards popped up, surrounding the popularity of Cabbage Patch Kids. They were gross-out bastardizations of the Cabbage Patch names and came with gum that nobody ever chewed. But this gift might as well have been a pair of diamond stud earrings. Garbage Pail Kids were as, if not more, valuable to a third grader. I would beg my disapproving Mensa level intellectual mom to take me to the Super D grocery store to buy them, mulling over which waxy package contained the gem I'd been searching for, maybe "Ground Chuck" or "Snotty Dotty." They were disgusting but they made you somebody before you even knew you needed to be somebody. Nathan was showing me I had value.

This letter and gift should have made me giggle and blush and stay up all night thinking about Nathan D. but it didn't. Nathan was romantically activated and he forced me to romantically activate as well. Nature and nurture had their chance and now I was out on my own, faced with deciding how I was going to play this boy vs. girl game. When Nathan made his move, instinctually I knew a guy who liked me couldn't possibly be good enough. Blame nature or nurture, but that's what came to the surface. I couldn't have put that into words then, but I never responded to Nathan. I ignored him and his longing looks through his bowl cut bangs. Because he was nice. And he liked me. And he wasn't afraid to tell me. I went back to liking Trampus Krane, who would never like me back. And a pattern was born. I recently went out with a smart, curious, motivated, shaggy haired guy in an argyle sweater, who invited me to the perfect bar, paid for my fancy throwback cocktail, and was interested in hearing all about me as I threw it back. He told me I looked nice in my large tortoise shell glasses but the whole time I kept thinking about a guy, who was far away in New York, who'd never bought me a fruity gin drink or told me I looked nice in my glasses or indicated really in any way that he liked me other than being able to finish when we had sex. I literally thought in my head, "Well, New York guy came, so I guess that means he likes me or he wouldn't have been able to finish, right?" His disinterest made me interested. Maybe it's like that for everyone though. Trampus Krane married the girl he chased around the halls of his high school for quite a while before she agreed to go out with him. I wonder if they're happy?

Nathan moved in the fourth grade and I never saw him again. I Googled his name. If he's still in Texas, he's either a Sunday school teacher, a paramedic—who recently helped deliver a baby at a minor league baseball game—or into some weird sex stuff. Maybe he's single. I'd like to tell him I still think of him and his red hair. I'd like to tell him he was the first person to tell me I was pretty. I'd like to send him a picture of me, resurrecting that lopsided smirk and ask for a do-over. It could have changed everything.

TRULY TASTELESS JOKES, OR HOW I LEARNED ABOUT SEX

My parents never taught me about sex. And unless they're waiting for my thirty-fifth birthday I don't think they're going to. Everything that I learned about sex, I learned on the street. I listened to older girls on the bus. I listened at slumber parties as girls talked about what they thought happened when people "did it." During one slumber party at a friend's house, whose pool, for the record, was a giant empty uncovered death trap in their backyard, we got into a heated debate. It was sixth grade and I was told I was going to hell because I thought I'd lose my virginity before I got married. My reasoning was that if it felt good, I would probably want to do it. In a heavily religious South Texas town, this did not go over well. Doing anything that feels good is mostly frowned upon. What did they know? They also spent all night lip-syncing to that Starship album with "We Built this City on Rock and Roll" on it because they didn't know it was bad yet. And I have no doubt someone at that party got pregnant before turning eighteen.

I was eager to learn about sex at that age, but the wells around me were running dry. Everyone's knowledge sort of started in the right place and ended in the right place, but was vague in the middle: "Everyone gets naked something, something, something, something then a baby is born." So, when my parents would go to bed, I'd sneak downstairs not to look in the golden edged pages of our soon-to-be-extinct Encyclopedia Britannica, but to watch HBO. Late night HBO showed rated R movies. And rated R movies showed S-E-X. The *Porky's* series was the best resource. I dissected every scene. I knew guys liked boobs. I knew guys did something to themselves when they saw boobs. I knew I would get boobs and hard nips and something called a puss (like *Puss in Boots*) or pussy (like pussywillow). I'd try to piece together all the clues I had but there were still giant gaps in my sexual knowledge. How does the penis interact with the vagina? Does it have anything to do with a girl's period or tampon or maxipad? Do babies come out of butts or pee holes? How many holes are down there? There were more questions than there were answers. And there was nobody to ask. Then, the second happiest accident, after the discovery of penicillin, occurred at our local bookstore in Sunrise Mall; B. Dalton's.

I'd gone to the store with my mom for a totally separate reason. I knew I wasn't the cutest, smartest, or most athletic girl in the sixth grade and it was starting to show so I needed something. A hook.

Just a little explanation here, I was in a Gifted and Talented magnet program for elementary school, where we had our own school, but when we got into middle school we were bused across town to a school in an "at risk" neighborhood. A neighborhood with drug- and gun-sniffing dogs, a pot-dealing ice cream truck driver, and gangs. Gangs, in *sixth* grade. And pregnant girls. In the *sixth* grade. Our school district in general has so many pregnant teens it has a separate campus called T.A.M.S. (Teenage Mother's School). This was very confusing when the city renamed our local University Texas A&M at Corpus Christi, T.A.M.U.C.C.

I distinctly remember walking through the main hall of my middle school dressed as a princess for our program's Renaissance Faire holding a balsa wood replica of Notre Dame I'd made complete with Rose Window, and realizing I wasn't in Kansas anymore. Electives and P.E. were the only classes we had with the "regular" kids. That's what the school called the kids who weren't in the gifted program. The "regular" kids didn't like us. I wonder why. And everyone had a different way of handling the contempt. I decided to try and become their wacky P.E. buddy. For a while, I wore mirrored sunglasses with palm trees on them and sang pop songs like Salt-n-Pepa's "Push It" in a classic "what's this crazy white girl doing" routine but it wasn't enough. I needed jokes.

Funny was going to be my hook. So, at B. Dalton's I bought a few books in a series that sounded promising: Truly Tasteless Jokes. There is nothing thirteen-year-old kids are if not tasteless. I don't know why my mother allowed this purchase but she was in graduate school then so maybe she was just too tired to care or maybe she knew I needed a hook too. I went home ready to learn some zingers I could pull out the next time I was forced on some regular kid's flag football team. The first section was full of quadriplegic jokes.

> Q: What do you call a guy with no arms and no legs in the
> middle of a field during a lightening storm?
> A: Rod.

Other sections were similar. There were dead baby jokes, Helen Keller jokes, Jewish jokes, WASP jokes, and Polish jokes. I had never met a Polish person. In Texas they were called Aggie jokes—after the Texas A&M Aggies.

> Q: Why do Aggies/Pollocks hate M&Ms?
> A: They are too hard to peel.

Needless to say, my plan to make myself well liked through jokes was clearly coming true. Then I got to the male and female anatomy chapters and the happy accident revealed itself. Truly Tasteless Jokes are how I came to learn everything I needed to know about sex. Thank you, Volumes 1–4. Every night, I snuck away right after dinner to examine the books under my dinosaur sheets so nobody would catch me. Figuring out what I was reading was like doing a math equation. "Okay, if A equals penis then B equals cunt. What's a cunt?" I'd flip frantically to find another joke that had the word cunt in it. "Oh, cunt equals vagina!" It was the un-sexiest way to learn about sex but at least I was learning. There was one joke I will never forget:

A maid was cleaning up the honeymoon suite at a
hotel. There was a note scribbled out and left on the bed.
It said, "Sorry about the mess." The maid finished the
room, made the bed, and left the couple a note: "It's okay.
Please cum again."

Cum. C-U-M. I had never heard that term before. I took it apart just like I would diagram a sentence in Mrs. Boone's English class. Please. Cum. Again. Dirty sheets. Post-honeymoon. A man and a woman. Bride and groom. Please come again. But not come. C-U-M. I didn't get it. Why the superfluous "u"? Then I read some more jokes about "giz" and white stuff that seemed to come out of a man's "dick," "cock," "wanker," "Johnson." Johnson. Big Johnson shirts! I finally got it. Johnsons make cum. Cum is white and gooey and tastes bad according to these jokes. Women swallow it or spit it out. Men can't stop it from happening. They sometimes put it in socks or their hand or a Kleenex. A condom catches this stuff. It also has sperm in it. Sperm makes a baby. Man. It was all coming together. A man has sperm come out of his penis and it spills everywhere. That's why they felt bad for the maid. She had to clean up gooey white sperm from the groom's penis. It was on the sheets! He CUMMED on the SHEETS!

Years of *Porky's* jokes finally made sense. I got it. I knew that a man rubbed his penis on a woman's breasts ("tits," "ta-tas," "fun bags," "boobies"), then put it in a woman's vagina ("cunt," "pussy," "hole," "twat," "gash"), and that white stuff ("cum," "giz," "spooge," "spunk," "baby batter," "discharge") came out and made a baby. I was unstoppable. I could take on any girl at the back of the bus with her misinformation and brother's *Adam & Eve* sex toy catalog. I could fill in that something something something. I finally knew what got girls into T.A.M.S. I was an encyclopedia of sex terms and dirty joke punch lines. I just didn't know what to do with them, yet.

I KNOW YOU'RE IN THERE, WHORE!

I was sweet and sixteen when I saw that Jezebel naked with my boy-friend, Gregory, on top of her in his unmade bed in his backyard trailer through those cheap metal blinds. She was a senior and I was devastated. I wondered if he told her that he'd go slow too. Probably not. She probably wanted it fast and hard, not slow and soft like a stupid baby. She probably didn't shake with nervousness when he touched her. In fact, I knew she tied up our friend Steve with scarves. One on each bedpost. In high school! I wondered what kind of underwear she wore. It probably wasn't white with little bows and bought at the Carter's children's clothing store by her mother. They were thongs for sure. Probably leopard print. Slut. After taking it all in, I started to bang on the trailer door and yell and scream and lose my mind.

"I know you're in there . . . whore. I see you!"

Love doesn't always end up where it begins, but everyone has to learn that for themselves. That lesson came before I could vote. In high school, my best friends and I hung out at a twenty-four-hour coffee shop painted to look like a barn. Inside, the walls were covered in rusty antique animal traps. It was called Harvey's Barn Door and sadly it has now closed (maybe a victory for public health). Harvey's had roaches and cheap nachos, endless cups of coffee and endless hours of conversation about pretentious German philosophers from kids who weren't cheerleaders or jocks and hence didn't have much use for the Texas high school scene. I smoked cigarettes out of boredom—the profound boredom of living in a sleepy town where people's values were all screwed up. Where cheerleaders and football players were kings and queens, but in private got drunk and got abortions. I despised the kids who were grandfathered into popularity because of their name or money, but yet just like any of those aspiring Homecoming Queens I detested, all I really wanted to do was to fall in love. And I did. With Gregory.

We met through mutual friends on the debate team. I was a wide-eyed high school freshman and he was a wide-eyed college freshman, which is why he liked coming home. At home, he was the cool guy. The college guy. The high school debate legend. The lady-killer. At college I'm guessing he wasn't. Since I had been kiss-less and boyfriend-less up until the point I met Gregory I didn't know that he was flirting with me. I didn't know that behind the scenes there were negotiations between a few of his friends over who would get a crack at me. Wow, did I have the world by its balls and not even realize it. Gregory was concerned about our age difference. Called me jailbait. Lolita. But he called me. And we went on our first date in his Nissan Pulsar that had ants. And a few weeks later, when summer came, my friends and I hung out in the trailer, where he lived in his backyard (it was Texas), and talked about things we didn't know anything about and about the people we thought we were but really just wanted to be. And I fell, hard.

I'd heard about love, but until Gregory I didn't know what it was. He inspired me to write lame poetry entitled, "His Blue-Gray Eyes" and "Eight Months," which I found buried in a box under my childhood bunk-beds last year. I won't bore you with all eight pages, handwritten on legal pad with a number two pencil. But here's one of my favorite parts:

> "I have fallen in like with you. But really when I say that I mean I've fallen in love with you. That scares me. I know like. I love you. I don't know love."

I thought Greg dated me for my intelligence not my looks but later he told me I wasn't that smart, which was a compliment and of course an insult. Gregory was my first real kiss. We were on the trampoline in his backyard next to his dad's vegetable garden.

"Are you nervous?" he asked, as we rested at the center of the wet-from-dew trampoline. I wanted to die because I was so nervous, but at the same time I felt like I would kill myself if he didn't kiss me. Some complex feelings for a sweet, simple, teenage Republican.

"Yes," I squeaked out.

"I'll go slow," he assured me. And he did. I was shaking. I didn't know what to do with my lips, my mouth, my teeth, my tongue! It was too much. I felt like running away all the way down his block and through the large field and low income housing with a high-income name like Royal Bluffs that separated our neighborhoods. I wasn't ready for this, but I wanted it so bad. After a few times I loosened up . . . sort of. A million things that have no business zinging around in my head during a first kiss began zinging. Whether or not I had to pee. Will I ever go to Hawaii? Am I fat? Do I floss enough? Will I get cancer?

Gregory and I progressed to more than just kissing. I didn't really understand what that entailed. I knew from my Truly Taste-less Jokes book that his penis would get hard. Become "an erection" ("a woody," "boner," "a hard on," "a tent pole in his pants"). I would fumble around and rub on his belt for a while until I realized I was nowhere close. I think I gave his belt some pretty good hand jobs if I may say so myself. I liked rubbing his chest and I liked it when he touched my boobs. I'd never really felt my boobs being felt before. He told me my nipples were different, brown. I didn't know they came in any other color. He said most are pink. I'd never really seen anyone else's nipples up close, and I'd never had anyone critique my body in any way. My body was as new to me as it was to him. He said his favorite part of a woman was the drop from her hips to her waist. He stroked this part of me over and over again but he hadn't discovered it on me. After fooling around a few times he told me I couldn't wear little girl underwear anymore because it made him feel weird (but the fact that he was in college and I was in high school didn't make him feel weird). I didn't even know I wore little girl underwear. It was cotton and white with bows on the front. I guess he was right. But nobody had seen it before to comment.

Not long after that first kiss, and that first innocent fondling, we had sex (in the trailer). There was nothing remarkable about it and I don't mean it as an insult to him. I wanted to "get it over with." I wanted to join the ranks of the sexually active. It's like going camping. It's fun to tell people you camp, even though you don't really enjoy it while you're doing it. I laid completely still during "sex." He'd had it before so he knew what he was doing. It was still awkward though getting the parts to match up correctly. We only exchanged two sentences. He said, surprised, "It's not in. That's why it didn't feel right. Why didn't you tell me?" I was confused and just said, "I didn't know."

When it was in, I felt a lot of physical pressure and not much else. I did love him but this event and that love didn't seem to have anything in common. Then he went back to his college smack dab in the middle of Texas farmland. And I didn't hear from him that much. I sent care packages with honey buns and decorated letters with intricate marker drawings of Hunter S. Thompson (who he loved) and local newspaper clippings of interest, just like a doting grandmother. And just like a grandmother, I knew when he opened them he had to think of me. I filled my student planner (which I still have) with the dates he'd be back in town marked with colorful stickers of things like Teenage Mutant Ninja Turtles that I'd bought at a more innocent time. I talked endlessly about how in love I was with Gregory to bored friends, who I'd dumped for him. I ceased to do much living on my own and began waiting. Something I'm ashamed I also do in adulthood. There's nothing like that feeling of waiting for a guy. It's the loneliest feeling in the world. Holding that cell phone in your hand as you take out the trash, use the bathroom, change the litter box. Fearful that the one second you aren't looking will be when they call. Pathetic. And something I have done as recently as last week. What I do know now, and didn't know then, was that no relationship that makes you feel that insecure lasts. You aren't really waiting for a phone call; you're waiting for the other shoe to drop.

And it did. Gillian was a few years older than me, an artist and self-proclaimed "atheist" who oozed sexuality with her full bangs and bra-lessness in white men's v-necks. She drove without shoes. She was so wild. I knew she always had a crush on Gregory. Part of her crush was wanting what we had. I knew she was more right for him. And one night everyone knew. A bunch of us had gone to see *Hoffa* at the movie theatre. Gregory barely acknowledged me. This man, who I'd kissed on that wet trampoline. This man I'd had awkward un-wet first sex with. He sat next to her, I sat in Siberia. I don't remember a single scene of the movie. I spent the entire movie staring at her eating her overly buttered popcorn. She might as well have been devouring tiny morsels of my broken heart. Gregory had showed me what half of all love songs were about. The beginning. The butterflies. But now he was showing me what the other half were about. Betrayal. Hatred. Pain.

After the movie, we went back to a friend's house to drink. White Russians to be exact. I finished one or maybe even half and was blitzed. I was sixteen; it wasn't possible to have a lower tolerance. Gregory and the artist slipped out when I was in the bathroom. I knew they were going back to the trailer. And so shortly after I followed. Halfway there I realized I wasn't okay to drive. There's no excuse for this except that I was sixteen and dumb.

When I got to Gregory's house, it was dark. I knew the lock on his front door didn't work for shit, so with a hard twist I was in. His parents were sleeping. I crept past their room, treading lightly on the Saltillo tile and past the kitchen where I found his younger brother, a football player at my rival high school, in his plaid boxers eating holiday leftovers and drinking a Dr. Pepper.

I was furious, like a crazy love-struck teenager who has just broken into the house of the guy she lost her virginity to who is now presumably banging her full-banged friend.

"They're out there aren't they?!"

His brother said he didn't know and wished me a Merry Christmas (good kid). He asked if Gregory knew I was coming over. His family was close and even in a moment of panic he tried to protect Gregory. I threw the back door open and let myself into the cold backyard, down the cement path to the trailer past the trampoline where I had my first kiss and finally understood what everyone in the history of the world was talking about. I put my ear to the door and peeked in the window. Then I saw them. I started to yell curse words at random. "Dammit! Fuck! Asshole! Mother! Shit! Whore!" I wasn't yet adept at stringing them together. Gregory could not ignore the cries of a sixteen-year-old in little girl underwear scorned for the first time in her life. He started to pull on his khaki Dockers and came to the door. I called the artist out by name and screamed, "I hope you're fucking ashamed of fucking!"

The only thing I could think to do was run. I ran through the house, past his brother in the kitchen, past the broken lock on the front door with a folksy wreath welcoming you in. I could feel White Russian swirling in my head and stomach and bowels. I got into my SUV wondering how I'd drive stick shift (couldn't have sprung for the automatic, Dad!) while crying my fucking heart out. Because I was crying so badly and hyperventilating I couldn't get a scream to come out so I just kept honking the horn. Long, short. Short, long. Neighbors turned on lights. Then I saw her. She came running out putting his oversized Oxford shirt on and took off. Gregory followed and begged me with large animated gestures to stop honking. Tears shot out of my eye ducts like the Water Willy we used to have in our yard in the summertime. But that was what I wanted. His attention. And I had gotten it. I unlocked the car door. My tears found his knit Polo that smelled like her. The neighbors' lights stayed on so we decided to go somewhere else. Just him and me. That was all I wanted. Us.

We drove to a Texan Star convenience store a few minutes away. The same place where he would buy my lottery tickets since I was underage. Not old enough to buy lottery tickets but young enough to be destroyed like this. He didn't say anything really. I didn't say anything because I wanted him to like me still and all I could think of were horrible friendship/relationship ending things. "You're a selfish pig slut." "You're a liar." "I wish I hadn't lost my virginity to you." I wanted more than anything for it to be like it was. The little girl underwear. Our inside jokes. That look that he only gave me. Or that I hoped he only gave me. Black Sabbath was on the radio.

It took another four years but eventually that pain faded away. Gregory taught me about love, sweet and bitter, but when I think back about that time, where he'd eclipsed everything in my life, it's not the love or the heartache that comes up. That had to happen in order for me to join the ranks of humanity. What I think about now, is that trailer in Gregory's backyard. When I see him now, there's no trace of those feelings I once had, but when his family got rid of that trailer I realized I was still quite attached. I was really sad. My real love affair was with that trailer, a hub of youth. A place where we were all trying to figure out who we were without parental supervision. It's where I became a woman and not because I lost my virginity there. We explored new ideas and defended old ones. We fought about politics and comedy. We found out the difference between tipsy and drunk. We found out what made us laugh would later make us cry. We wore cut-off short shorts because we fit in them. We did nothing, because we could. I wish I could go back in time and be in that trailer with my friends before any bad things happened to us. Or good things happened to us. Before we met other friends in other places and realized maybe we were just friends because we were the only like-minded people in an un-like-minded Texas town. I wish we could have one more night of cheap beer, wine coolers, and easy conversation. We could smoke and not be smokers. We could drink and not be drinkers. We could love and not be suckers. We could dream and not be losers. It was such a beautiful time. Everything was possible because we didn't know anything yet. And I remember that trailer a lot more than I do that "whore," who is probably a lovely person, living a non-whore life out there in the world somewhere. But we still don't have to be friends. And who knows, maybe she is a whore.

HEY, BABY, LET ME SEE YOUR TATTOO!

The first real job I ever had was working as an assistant at a computer consulting firm, Compu-Daze, forty hours a week, which at sixteen felt like labor camp hours. We were in poorly lit, neutral colored offices, with stained carpets above the Rim Shot jazz bar and dance club. It was eighteen and over but it could have been eighty and over and the clientele wouldn't have changed.

The short-sleeved button up wearing husband and chubby good-natured wife who started the company began with nothing but their state school educations and student loans and ended up with a successful business and a teal colored Sea-Doo. They even got to bring their beloved gray parrot to work, who had a big chicken wire cage in our main room that looked like it was built in a junior high shop class by a kid who failed the assignment. The pet parrot wasn't that smart though and could only say:

"Hey, baby let me see your tattoo."

He used those seven words to express every emotion he had. He'd always get stuck on words. For example, he would start:

"Hey, baby. Hey, baby. Let me see your tattoo tattoo tattoo tattoo tattoo!" Then he'd fly wildly around the cage as he screamed, "Tattoo! Tattoo! Tattoo!"

Being a receptionist there was like being a kid with a drunk mom. I was constantly making excuses about the ridiculous scream-ing and banging in the background.

Only two other women worked there, Gloria and Justine. Gloria was the first Italian person I'd ever met. She had dark skin, deep rich brown eyes, and slick black hair. I asked if she was Hispanic. For some reason that offended her. She said she was so poor growing up that she ate dandelions. Her mother would present it like a game and she and her sister tried to collect as many as they could. She used to work in a window factory with Justine, and that's where they became friends. Justine had hair that didn't know if it was trying to be long or short, which was a color that didn't know if it was blonde or red and wore jeans pulled up high around her low boobs.

Gloria and Justine were more different than any women I'd met before. I loved how honest they were with me. I'd never met adults like that because I came from a world where adults closed doors to have important conversations and arguments and tell the truth. But they were the opposite. They would get in screaming fights in the middle of the office. It was great. Sometimes it seemed like they were one insult away from pulling off their fake fingernails and going toe to toe.

One day, when the summer was ending and it was almost time for me to go back to high school, they pulled me aside. They'd sent the guys out to get lunch, and I was nervous that they were going to fire me with only two weeks of summer left. But then they started to giggle. I sat down in a rolling office chair.

Gloria pulled me toward them and said, "We want to talk to you about something."

Justine nodded. "It's *really* important." The parrot wanted to get in on the action. He screeched, "Hey, baby . . ."

Gloria laughed, then tried to collect herself and "get serious."

Wait. Maybe they *were* firing me.

Gloria began slowly. "Justine and I have been talking about it and there's something we think you need to know, you know, as you become an adult. It might be the most important thing you need to know in life."

I thought about the books kids get for graduation, like *Oh, The Places You'll Go* and all the crap you read in graduation cards. "Follow your dreams." "Chase the stars." "Find your passion." I waited for their particular version, ready to nod politely, and then promptly forget.

Justine leaned in, "You see, everything you want in life you can get one way . . ."

Gloria finished her thought. "By giving a great blow job."

Instantly I turned the kind of bright red kids' plastic lunch boxes come in. I had only heard my parents cuss a handful of times. I wasn't even allowed to say damn in my house and these grown women were talking to me about blow jobs! I'd had bad sex a few times but I didn't even fully understand what a blow job was at that point. The whole idea was way too advanced and intimate. More intimate than sex for me. Truly Tasteless Jokes had a whole chapter on blow jobs, but was unclear on exactly how logistically they were performed. Do you just blow on it? Blow into it?

As these and several million other questions raced through my head, I managed to say, "Uh-huh."

Justine continued. "A man can be completely controlled by a woman who gives a great blow job. It's a skill you *must* learn."

Gloria used her hand to simulate a quite large penis in retrospect. "You have to take it deep. That's the secret."

OK, I thought, *you do actually put it in your mouth.*

The two women proceeded to show me their blow job techniques (apparently there was swallowing involved), while the boys were out

39

innocently picking up turkey sandwiches on warm freshly made white bread and the parrot screamed to show him my tattoo. "Tattoo, tattoo, tattoo! Hey, baby!"

This conversation freaked me out so much I didn't give a blow job until my sophomore year of college. It was to a Rabbi's son named Moishe Ethan Goldfarb. And it wasn't without the faint ringing of "Tattoo. Tattoo. Tattoo" in my head.

THE CASE OF THE
REALLY TIGHT H.J.

In high school I spent a lot of time at the local music store, The Record Factory, which didn't really sell records anymore. I'd walk up and down the aisles looking for the Nice Price CDs and admiring the long-haired guy who worked there, Mr. Record Factory Guy. He was a white hippie surfer with perfect eyebrows and unnaturally blue eyes that looked like someone took the ocean down to Home Depot's paint department and had them match it. After so many trips to Record Factory that I was worried my checks would start bouncing, it finally happened. He came over and talked to me while I was perusing the jazz section, holding a Charles Mingus CD in my hand. His name was Derrick. "So, you like Charles Mingus?"

"Of course. He's the best."

I barely knew anything about Charles Mingus or jazz but I knew it was cool and liking it made me cool. He said he owned the Mingus box set and would copy it for me from tape to tape. It would take him hours. At seventeen that was like someone offering to fly you to Paris for the weekend.

Derrick got my phone number off my check (which was wildly romantic) and called to tell me when it was ready. I met him at closing time, in the parking lot. He'd cut his long hair off. He'd needed a change. We sat and talked in the back of his teal green pick-up truck and after an hour of getting to know each other, with Sunrise Mall in the background, he kissed me and I had my second boyfriend. I was Mrs. Record Factory Guy . . . almost.

I was a sophomore when we met and he was a twenty-three-year-old graduate student at the local University studying Marine Biology. He was sweet and simple and optimistic. I think he might have been the first optimist I'd ever met. He saw beauty in things nobody else did. He used to drop by my mom's office at the University to check-in. This allowed us to date despite the age difference because he "seemed like such a nice boy." And he was.

Derrick had a tattoo of his ex-girlfriend's initials on his back. He got them when he was twenty. See, optimism. We used to drive out to the oil refineries at night and stare at their blinking orange lights and billowing smoke, because it was free and because it was spectacular in a way I wouldn't appreciate until I left South Texas. He played music for me I'd never heard, obscure jazz and surf. He made me pot brownies. He bought me knee socks. He told me I had value as a woman and a person. He listened to me. I'd never met a guy who really listened to me. He told me I was pretty.

I used to skip school and meet him at his English-Tudor-style-if-I-had-to-guess apartment complex on Ocean Drive (only in Corpus Christi could ocean front property cost less than two-hundred dollars a month and involve fake turrets). These field trips were about being alone together in his bed with mismatched sheets, when mismatched sheets didn't matter to me. When his half-brother/roommate wasn't around. When my parents weren't wondering where I was.

I didn't want to have sex with more than one guy while I was in high school, so I waited to have sex with Derrick until I graduated.

That seemed lady-like. So, for the first chunk of our relationship my focus was hand jobs because I certainly wasn't ready for blow jobs. But I was confused about how to give hand jobs. Really confused. I would hold on really tight and go at it super fast. Tight and fast. Sometimes his hand would meet mine and slow it down. I didn't pick up on the signals. One day during a typically tight hand job he jerked and pulled away.

"Owwwwww! Too tight!"

I was humiliated. I didn't like doing things wrong. I wished I'd never pretended to like Charles Mingus. I decided I would leave that afternoon and never see him again. He knew he upset me. He knew I was a perfectionist. But Derrick was gentle and understanding. And made me remember I *was* a teenager, I was supposed to make mistakes. He might worry if he was dating a seventeen-year-old who gave perfect hand jobs. He ran his fingers through my hair that was becoming a dirtier blonde each year and let me talk when I was ready.

"I thought it was supposed to be tight. I thought tight was good?"

"It can be good. It can also be too tight."

"But in rap songs and stuff they say 'tight' and it's a good thing. Vaginas are supposed to be tight and aren't I imitating a vagina with my hand." Always logic oriented.

"I think you just got confused. That's okay. Even bad ones feel pretty good."

The hip hop and rap community had misled me. If it were a Nancy Drew book it would have been called, *The Case of the Really Tight H.J.* I was glad we got that cleared up but probably not as glad as he was. But more importantly I was glad he helped me start a conversation about sex. I'd had a boyfriend before. I'd had sex before but not a conversation about what we were doing. Not a conversation about what usually happened in the dark under covers with a guilty conscience. Derrick opened me up and taught me sex could happen in the light of day and that saying the word "orgasm" would only make me stronger. He was the first person that made me feel like sex wasn't embarrassing or shameful. I can thank him for a lot of positive sexual experiences in my life when I was able to ask for what I wanted, and in a way I can thank him for my career. If you can't write a good dick joke, you can't make it as a comedy writer and to do that you have to be able to say the word "dick" out loud.

I dated Derrick until Christmas of my freshman year of college. I broke up with him after I cheated with someone who never told me I was pretty, or made me twenty Charles Mingus cassette tapes or cared if I said "orgasm" let alone had one. There have been a lot of drunken nights in my life when I've done things I've regretted but never as much as I regretted hurting him.

I haven't talked to Derrick in a long time but I'm jealous of the woman he's married to. I know she can't do any wrong, because in his ocean blue eyes she's perfect just the way she is no matter what kind of hand jobs she gives.

HE DIDN'T EVEN
LOOK AT ME TWICE

I interned at the White House from October of 1994 to January of 1996. He didn't even look at me twice. All I got was a lousy tote bag and a box M&Ms with the Presidential seal on them. When the Lewinsky scandal broke, I'm not going to lie, my feelings were a little hurt.

AUSTIN POWERS, JR.

At the end of college I dated a graduate student from American University. His name was Pat. He had red hair. Not the orange kind. But the kind that seemed angry. He drank too much. He wore bright unnaturally colored fleece and khaki shorts like they were his uniform. I was in total like with him. We started "dating," which meant when he was done at the trying-too-hard-to-look-old bar he worked at, I would come over and have a beer/cider while he cleaned up. He worked at a bar near Gallaudet, a deaf college, and the deaf drunk people would get really rowdy and start fights. Took a while to notice because they didn't make much noise. After he cleaned up the bar and kicked the deaf kids out, we would go back to his house and have sex. Him on top. Me totally silent. Missionary only. I was so uncomfortable in my own skin I couldn't even enjoy sex. One time he told me, "We can do it a different way if you want." I said, "It doesn't matter." I would just lie there and tell myself, "You're doing it. You're really having sex. That's what adults do to have fun." When I was growing up, one of my uncles had a magnet on his fridge that said, "I (HEART) Sex." I finally got it. Side note, I wish I had a sex do-over with Pat just so I could show him that I finally learned a few more positions.

Pat had this mean Husky who bit me hard one night while Pat was in the bathroom. My right hand. He bit my hand as I reached out to pet him. I pretended like it was totally fine as I bled everywhere.

"It doesn't hurt at all. Just stings a little really."

I still have a scar, which is almost as bad as having a tattoo of an ex-boyfriend's name on your arm. As long as I have my hand, I will never forget Pat or his stupid dog, Monkey.

I met Pat almost a year after *Austin Powers* came out, but I was just back from study abroad and figuring out what I was doing for the summer and I totally missed the entire craze. I was pretty involved on campus and never really went to the movies. I'd heard people talk about it but I'd never seen it. Never heard the catch phrases or now looking back on it, I had heard the catch phrases I just didn't know what they'd come from. So, enter Pat.

Pat was a friend of a friend I met on study abroad in Vienna, Austria. He'd recently moved to D.C. and after meeting for some friendly-face-in-a-new-town drinks, we started hooking up. He seemed like a guy who was bad for me and our mutual friends warned me but I couldn't resist. He was hilarious. Goddamn hilarious. Pat used to always say things like, "Are you randy, baby?," and pull down his shirt to reveal his auburn chest hair. Or put his pinky to his mouth and say, "It will cost one hundred billion dollars." He was filled with these comic gems. I was blown away. He was a genius. He would crack me up with his British accent. Was I "horny"?! I was now. He called his smaller best friend "Mini Me." A one-man comedy show! I couldn't get enough. Wasting that kind of funny on a career in medicine? Inexcusable.

Then *Austin Powers* came out on VHS. One late night after some beers and right-priced tacos we watched it and everything came together. The billion dollars. The "Mini Me." The "Scoooooooott" in a German accent. The comic genius I was dating was just the annoying guy who repeats phrases from hit movies like, "Alllllrightly then" and "Schwing"! I was humiliated. I wanted to get on my hands and knees, crawl out the door, and never look back. I'd told all my friends, friends who were planning on dedicating their lives to comedy, that he was one of the funniest guys I had ever met. That night, while we were having sex, I convinced myself it was okay. Remember, I had low self-esteem. At least he did a good impression, but I didn't laugh at his "Let's shag, baby" jokes anymore.

Watching *Austin Powers* had killed it for both of us. If it hadn't come out on VHS we might be married right now.

Wherever you are, Pat, I hope you are randy.

MY GAY EX–BOYFRIENDS

When I was younger, I was attracted to gay guys and they were "attracted" to me. I don't exactly know why. Maybe they took things slower. Maybe they looked nice and showered. Maybe they were interested in activities other than drinking beer and watching sports. Maybe they took time to get to know me when other heterosexual guys were just interested in sex (in high school one of my best guy friends told me all he was looking for was a "greasy hole"). Maybe after my first real relationship, where there was cheating, betrayal, and jealousy, I was just looking for something easier, a situation where I was in control. But it turned out the gay guys were the ones holding all the cards, both physically and emotionally, and I've certainly paid the price for making that mistake. And so have all the guys I've dated since. But allow me to introduce you to the exes:

GARRETT
When: High School
Garrett doesn't deserve much of a mention though he was the first gay guy I slept with. My gateway gay. I was seventeen. It was New Year's Eve. I was at a college party in Austin, hours from where I lived and miles away from the kind of party my parents thought I was at. People were bonging beers, doing whippets, and getting the kind of

drunk you only get when you're young and have never had a hangover or a job. I used Garrett to make another guy jealous and he used me to see if he liked women. Neither worked. We slept together in bed that night and did nothing but sleep.

CRAIG

When: College

Craig was younger than me but really cute in a young-Peter Gallagher way. He had dark defined eyebrows and a barely-there goatee. The only thing wrong with him was his Tevas, but America was still in its Teva love affair. We were both Resident Assistants at GW, so we stayed in town for the summer and our "like" affair blossomed. It took Craig so long to kiss me; my friends called it The Winston Cup, and they put money they didn't have to lose down. Eventually, the kiss happened and that naturally led to fooling around. Craig was very upfront about the fact that he didn't like blow jobs. He claimed he had a low sex drive but chain-smoked cigarettes like a man who was dying for an orgasm. Craig liked to get drunk and call his best friend from high school, who happened to be a dude. This didn't seem right. The dude was a tennis player, with bleached blonde hair from spending so much time in the sun. According to Craig, this tennis player was the "funniest, smartest, coolest" guy. I met him once and he was okay. He was of average funny, smart, and cool. Craig would almost be in tears describing their intense friendship. All of this should have been suspect but then again he *was* from California. In my family "California" is a euphemism for everything weird and liberal. Craig happened to have a birthday the same week as mine, so we celebrated by going to see *Rent.* He was a musical theatre loving, best guy friend loving, not blow job loving virgin who didn't want to have sex. Remember I didn't have a lot of life experience.

Finally, after a few weeks I got up the courage to ask him, "Have you ever thought that maybe you're gay?"

Craig turned red with embarrassment and quickly blurted out, "No."

He implied that maybe *I* was the problem. My low self-esteem agreed, he was out of my league, and everyone, including him, now knew it. I was not pretty enough, sexy enough, or good enough in bed. I beat myself up thinking about what I could have done differently. Ice cube blow job. Victoria's Secret push-up bra. Red lipstick. Liposuction. Anorexia. This break-up haunted me for a long time.

In 2007 I got the following voice mail message . . .

Craig in a sing-songy voice, "Hello, Hilary. It's Craig. I'm living in L.A. I heard you were out here. Oh, and yes you were right. I *am* gay."

I played the message for astonished fellow writers at work, who were sure I had embellished my gay love story. Craig and I went to lunch. It's true. He's out. And a theatre director.

DANNY

When: Post-college/not yet an adult

Danny was still a senior at Yale when we met. He'd come out to L.A. to visit friends who were paving their way in the entertainment industry. He was hoping to follow that pavement the following May when he graduated. He had the confidence of an Ivy League guy. They're told they can do whatever they want and they believe it. Even if they're assistants, they know they're destined for success. I didn't know if I was destined for success so this confidence was a magnet.

After Danny went back to school we talked almost every day, our romance blooming over dial-up Internet and home phone lines. He was the reason I bought my first digital camera, which for the

most part was used for semi-naughty photos with well-placed graph-
ics. (They say porn drives the development of technology . . .) We'd
kissed, but never anything else, which was why I decided to fly out for
Valentine's Day. No pressure.

The first night I visited him on his intimidating campus, we had a
fancy Indian dinner with some of his friends. Indian seemed so sophis-
ticated for college kids, but of course it was Yale. His friends and their
SAT scores intimidated me so I had to work hard. Cracking jokes, finding organic ways to work in the impressive parts of my résumé: "When I
was at the White House . . ." "When I was working for Susan Stamberg
at NPR . . ." "While I was studying abroad in Vienna . . ." But at the end
of the day, which wasn't hopefully at the end of the day, I wanted to fool
around. I wanted to go back to his apartment, which was the large attic
of a small house, and have the kind of sex you fly across the country for.
I wanted it to be soft but hard. I wanted it to be slow but fast. I wanted
us to be animals but still hold each other. I wanted us to be Ali and Ryan
in *Lovestory*. I wanted to never have to say, "I'm sorry."

Back in his dorm room, he nervously caressed my hair, my face,
my small but perky breasts. I played my part. He removed my winter
clothes layer by layer. Purple wool jacket bought at a vintage store in
London. BR sale sweater. Heather gray turtleneck. White cotton tank
top like the kind moms make their little girls wear when they can't
admit their babies are ready for a bra. Finally we were both naked. No
phone lines to hide behind. No dot com. No pixels. I felt pretty. I felt
sexy. He made me feel this way. But he couldn't get it up. And by "it"
I mean his penis. He said it was stress, anxiety, but I knew that it was me
again. There was that self-hating voice in my head that said, "I told you.
Why would he want to have sex with you? Something is wrong with you.
Why do you try to pressure guys into having sex?" It didn't happen the
next night either and I was back on a plane without my love story.

Danny visited me once more in L.A. It was the same sexual excuses every day. Tired. Full from garlic knots and pasta. Wanted to make sure to get enough sleep so he would have enough energy for Disneyland. His last night at my place, I tried to come on to him, while we were watching my miniature TV that was perched on falling apart IKEA furniture. I put my hand down his pants. Instead of a happy groan, he said in an extremely firm tone, "Don't you see I'm trying to watch *Stir of Echoes.*" He wanted to watch a Kevin Bacon movie about a retarded girl getting raped more than he wanted to fool around with me. I was angry. I was sad. I was hurt. I was confused. I was defeated.

I never wanted to talk to him after that. I didn't return his phone calls. His fake e-mails. His fake emotions. His fake kisses and intentions. Maybe it was cruel. Maybe I should feel sorry for someone carrying such a heavy burden but I didn't. I was mad at gay men. Mad at them for introducing me as evidence to their parents (I'd met Craig's and Danny's) and their friends. It isn't a victimless crime.

Our mutual friends judged me for cutting Danny off. But it wasn't my place to tell them their friend was gay. Though it was his place to tell me.

Danny never came out to me. I never actually saw him again after his *Stir of Echoes* trip and I only talked to him once. We got into an argument about how I thought it sounded girly that he was going to have a slumber party with his guy friends, make ice cream sundaes and talk about their problems. Yeah, exactly. I did however get confirmation from a mutual friend of him canoodling under a blanket at a party with another guy. Unless *Stir of Echoes* was playing under that blanket, it's good enough evidence for me.

JAMES

When: Post-college/not yet an adult

James was a scam artist. A poser. A creep. He lied his way into every relationship he's ever had. Friendship. Roommates. Bosses. Parents. I didn't trust a word that came out of his mouth, eventually. We worked at the Paramount lot together. Both interns. The only difference was that I actually told people I was an intern. At first, I found his attitude intoxicating. Later I just found it toxic. He thought he could do anything and that anyone who knew him could do anything too. He knew how to get what he wanted. He tricked me into living with him when his roommate up and moved back to Montana, giving up the dream, and he was stuck without a place. He said it would just be for a few days and after a month I asked him about paying rent. Which he did start paying, sort of. He used his Ralph's club savings card at the supermarket (which they give you for free) and subtracted the amount he saved us from the rent he owed me because it was printed at the bottom of the receipt. One month, he couldn't pay rent so he opened up a Target credit card and took me on a shopping spree. He had several P.O. boxes, phones numbers, and, apparently, aliases. I'd notice credit card bills lying around from all sorts of places like Brooks Brothers. He didn't have that much money. We got a small stipend, certainly not a Brooks Brothers stipend, barely an Old Navy stipend. But maybe "Lyle Winthrop" had Brooks Brothers money.

I've never met anyone before who was so desperate to be famous in some way. He didn't know exactly how to do it, but he sure as hell wanted it. I can't tell you how many hours he spent sitting around that Paramount commissary waiting for someone to notice him. The only one who did, was me. Sucker.

One night, at a neighborhood bar called Birds, I think in order to impress the hot dude bartender, he told an elaborate story about how I'd moved out to Hollywood from D.C. to work on a show for the guy who created *Law & Order*, and that I had sold it to him based on my own experiences as a White House intern. It amazed and scared me. The ease at which he lied and enjoyed lying was remarkable. It seemed, along with clipping coupons and selling things he got for free on eBay, one of his strongest skills. His lying was on such a professional level it got me thinking about what my *Dateline* interview would sound like. Because the best liars always end up on *Dateline* I'd say, "I expected this from him. I saw it coming." I wouldn't pretend that he was nice and sweet and charming. I would say he was creepy and that we never talked about anything real. And that I *wished* he'd kept to himself and left me alone.

I was interning for a producer I will not identify in any way (you'll see why). The guy I worked for was bizarre and totally sexually harassed me. He'd pee with the door open. He'd tell me not to wear sweaters so he and the rest of my male coworkers could see my tits. Then one day he asked me if I liked it when my boyfriend fucked me. I paused. I should have been struck by how entirely inappropriate this was in a workplace situation. I should have been offended and stormed out and told him I would have my soon-to-be hired lawyers call his office.

Instead I sadly said, "No. He doesn't really fuck me all that much."

James and I had sex four times in four months. One time was after we watched a sexy Showtime late-night movie. I think James knew he was supposed to be "hot," "aroused," and ready for "intercourse" with his girlfriend after seeing bare-breasted chicks in knock-off *Star Wars* outfits get "sabered." We took a shower together and then as we dried off we started having sex in front of the bathroom mirror. So far, so good. Then I caught him running his fingers through his *own* hair, which ruined it.

I confronted him about the lack of sex one night. I found the courage and then blurted, "I think it's weird we don't have sex that much."

He was in the middle of reading a magazine. He looked up from the magazine but not at me. He paused and his attitude read annoyed. Annoyed in the way a parent is annoyed by a little kid's barrage of questions. Then in the most condescending tone he spoke.

"I don't want to get in the habit of having sex a lot since I don't know how long we're going to last."

He said it like it was so obvious and I was an idiot for not seeing it. And then that was the end of the discussion. And shortly thereafter, the end of us. His last night at my place, he wrote me a nice letter referencing inside jokes I didn't find funny anymore and left me with a parting gift, a used Caller I.D. box. At least then I could avoid his calls. With confidence, I can say it was all I got out of my relationship with James.

———

A few years later I was at a graduation dinner party for a friend and sat next to a very hot interesting psychology grad student, who was of course gay, and had also dated James. He had quite a few stories about obsession and mild stalking. Afterwards, I felt like signing over my Caller I.D. box. It seemed like he earned it too.

IN CONCLUSION
When: Now
I now hold every man in my life gay until proven otherwise. Recently I hooked up with a guy who didn't want me to give him a blow job because he was too sweaty from cooking all day, and another wanted a crock-pot for his birthday. This did not go over well with my friends, who know my history, and I don't blame them. We must all be vigilant.

I view my gay exes like a team of villains who stole my sexual self-esteem. For years I thought that you had to convince guys to have sex. That you had to earn sex. They would put it off for as long as they could and then they'd have to give in. I would say this is not the typical girl experience. Instead of fending off guys' curious hands, I was trying desperately to get those hands anywhere.

This is not a healthy dynamic between a man and a woman, and it's certainly a slap in the face when you are lying there naked and your boyfriend turns up the volume on a retarded girl rape scene to signal he's not interested. I think after these experiences I was determined to find a guy's guy. A guy, who watched and played sports. A guy who was better with electronics than emotions. A guy who wanted to have sex more than I did. A guy I could dote on, cling to, and marry. But I swung as far to the other side as I could get.

I found guys who loved themselves so much they couldn't possibly love me. I found addicts and introverts. I found sex without love. I found men who wanted virgin whores. I found guys who needed compliments not commitment. I found guys who expected me to thank them for spending time with me. I found guys whose attention I could not possibly hold. And I found guys I could focus on, so I didn't have to focus on myself. I blame my gay ex-boyfriends for passing me the ball but I'm the one who ran with it.

THE SHY POOPER

After leaving a job on good terms, it's customary to have an exit interview. This is an opportunity for the employer to gain information from the employee about what they can do better and vice versa. Each party is usually more honest under these circumstances, knowing they won't have to continue to work together. Seems counterintuitive but worthwhile nevertheless. One guy I dated, Ian, believed male/female relationships should have exit interviews. And he gave me one, late one night, a week after we broke up.

Sometime post-midnight an IM popped up on my computer screen. I'm sure there was a part of me that was waiting for it. It was Ian, wondering how I was doing. How I was feeling about the break-up? I crawled into the trap he'd set by typing, "I miss you."

He wouldn't drive over to my place, said it was too far (about 1.6 miles). I headed over to his after putting on the best don't-you-miss-this-butt outfit I could find and lint rolling the cat hair off of it. I hoped the IM came less from a horny place and more from a place where he realized he'd made a mistake. That's why most single men are on the Internet late at night, right? They're obsessing over the girl who got away and how they can become better men to win her back? That's what I thought. I hoped Ian sent the IM because he just couldn't wait until morning to tell me that he missed me. That he wanted me. That he loved me. That he knew from the moment he met me that I was "the one." There were so many unanswered questions in my life.

I was twenty-three and nervous that I should have gone to law school like my friends. What if my parents were right about writing? My mom called it "tacky." It wasn't a real job, was it? I felt like someone's life savings on black. But all I needed to be happy was stability in one area of my life and something to counteract the two cats. A boyfriend could do both. To me, having a boyfriend is like buying a really nice piece of furniture, the kind of piece that classes up the whole room.

Ian's bedroom smelled like boy (dirty laundry/smoke from last night's bar + deodorant – recently microwaved food item/last night's take-out = boy smell). Turned out the IM most certainly came from a horny place. We had sex. Well, he had sex. I performed like it was my final audition, sorry neighbors. When we were done, he grabbed my hand softly and began the exit interview.

"You want to know something? In the future, with guys you date, you should add in a little more ball-play."

"Okay. Thank you."

Thank you?! I don't know where that came from. But I'd never been in that situation before. It was presented like a gift, so "thank you" seemed like the right response. Thank you for the sex advice I'll use with my next boyfriend? I didn't give him any advice in return. I could have said there was stuff he didn't do for me but I didn't know what it was yet. A few years later, when I was a little more experienced, I could have given him a great exit interview. It would have started with, "You're lazy." And ended with, "But only the pinky."

I didn't know exactly what Ian meant by "ball-play" and I was too embarrassed to ask. I just held his balls in my hand for a few minutes after we talked. They were the first balls I'd ever held. They felt like small hard-boiled eggs wrapped in raw chicken skin. I had a loose gentle grip. He had no comment but didn't pull away. Was this what people called break-up sex? Then we fell asleep with very different visions dancing in our heads.

Ian was tall and freckly with the creepiest, sexiest pale blue eyes. When we first met, there was an undeniable attraction. It had been a while since a guy looked at me like he could imagine "doing it" with me. My last boyfriend was imagining "doing it" with other dudes. I'd have to convince my gay ex to have sex with me, which was a lot of work and a real blow to the old self-esteem. In short, when I met Ian, my standards were low.

Ian and I got to know each other through work. I was an assistant at a television studio. He was an assistant at a network. Natural enemies, who were forced to work together to make mediocre projects. It was the most watered down version of the Montagues and the Capulets but in my head still romantic. Our bosses were working on an ambitious series together in Prague. We got to know each other well over the phone, well before we met in person. Ian was from the North East but he was obsessed with the South. Really obsessed. He liked country music, shirts with snaps, grits, Flannery O'Connor, and shit-kickers (boots). This fascination felt more like a rejection of his WASPy upbringing than anything else. It's the easiest way to rebel against your family and still get money from them.

Ian and I had a several month long passionate, dramatic, push-pull, up-down relationship filled with poetry and tears and blame and depression. And poetry about tears and blame and depression. It was never going to last but I didn't know that at the time.

What eventually did us in was a trip to Prague. The producers needed my help (running errands for their wives) on location. He wasn't asked to go. He was five years older than me and we had the same job. We stayed in touch while I was there, with phone calls I couldn't afford, but he seemed distant. It's tough to act even *more* distant when you are already on the other side of the planet, but he managed to.

I was gone for two months but it wasn't hard to be faithful. The sexual proclivities of the Czech locals freaked me out. I dare you to be a single woman in the Czech Republic and not get hit on by a married couple. It was explained to me that during the Communist reign sex was the only thing that was theirs and they really owned it. Good for them. I bet their ball-play skills were excellent. But as far as I was concerned, they could save their ecstasy-fueled threesomes for someone else.

I'd hoped for a loving twosome upon my arrival home but Ian broke up with me the first night I was back. Over the phone. It seemed like if he was going to do it over the phone, he could have just done it when I was Prague. He called me while I was driving on the twisty dark parts of Sunset Boulevard. I answered my cell phone even though I really needed both hands to ensure I'd survive the drive. I asked if I could call him back. He seemed put out, so I stayed on.

The last time I called him from Prague I told him I bought him a gift. It was a statue of a distressed man with no genitals holding a stand for a large spherical candle—Eastern Bloc art. Ian's response was to tell me not to buy him any more gifts and then refused to forward the conversation in any way. It's a classic pre-break-up guy move. He drives you to the edge of the cliff and waits for you to jump. The conversation on the phone while navigating the sharp turns on Sunset and then the bright lights of the strip wasn't a shock. He told me I wasn't the girl he started dating. That was the thesis of his break-up. He cited two incidents:

One was our first date. He reminded me about the time when he picked me up in his brand-new parent-paid-for Audi station wagon and I asked him where we were going. With a smirk he said, "It's a surprise."

I said, "Oh, so you're going to be all hey-little-girl-let-me-show-my-world-to-you. I'm not into that. Just tell me where we're going." Apparently this got his fire burning.

The other incident happened a month into our relationship, when discussing where to go for a long weekend, he suggested Vegas or Santa Barbara. I didn't have an opinion. "Doesn't matter where we go as long as we're together." This, apparently, put his fire out.

"It's over."

He liked it when I was sassy and sarcastic. He didn't think loving and sweet fit me. I didn't know which pair of adjectives I was or which pair I wanted to be. He clearly didn't want to date me but he was addicted to me in some way. He was addicted to someone who listened to his drama, supported his lazy self-indulgent poetry, pampered his ego, and acted like it wasn't fucking bizarre how obsessed he was the South. He was also addicted to someone who was too young to know he was failing.

The morning after my exit interview, I stroked his back. I wished it were Saturday. I admired the crappy pencil drawing he had above his bed that was hung on his wall with binder clips and string. I hated the silly stick figures in it but I wanted to date a guy who appreciated art. The rest of his walls were stark white. But because the screens on his windows were dirty everything was tinged with a slight yellow in the daylight, even his weirdly long torso that I stroked.

He woke up. We stared at each other in silence. He played with my hair. I thought for sure he must have been noticing the special in me that only he saw. He must have been noticing the tiny bit of green in my brown eyes. He must have been noticing what he had been missing the last week since we broke up. I was sure that after a couple of hours in my arms he didn't want me fondling anybody else's balls. He had sleepy eyes and I thought about how many more mornings I would see them like that. I wondered if we were going to get married. I wondered if we did where it would be. East Coast or Texas? Would I take his last name? He smiled and I smiled. I thought, "Wow, holding his balls in my hands really worked! I can't wait to tell my friends."

Ian, with great intensity and purpose looked at me, touched my face and said, "Will you . . . be leaving for work soon? Because I need to take a shit and I can't do it with you in the apartment." He punctuated it with a pat on my back.

I guess I'd been way off. But what did I expect? After the exit interview, you've got to make your exit. That's the only way it works.

PART 3

BATHING

IN TANDEM

AKA

MY FIRST

ADULT

RELATIONSHIP

MY FIRST ADULT RELATIONSHIP

Kyle was my first adult relationship, and a *guy* guy. He played base-ball (shortstop). He couldn't talk about his feelings (any of them). His favorite movies involved men with muscles, guns, and no time to fail. He drank beer (cheap) and scotch (expensive) and called women "bitches." I had no idea he would later write a book about us but I guess in my head I was keeping notes too.

Our relationship status was made official in Las Vegas. We went there for the weekend and got a cheap room at the Riviera, which was full of smoke and convention goers. We were the youngest people there by forty years. While walking down the strip in the blazing sun, heading to dollar Craps (my game) at the Sahara, he asked me if we were boyfriend/girlfriend. My little heart, scarred from previous relationships, raced. I told him I thought so. He agreed. There was no Elvis to officiate, but it was still special. Our hands sweated with heat or excitement or both. Then we went to Circus Circus where he won me a bunch of stuffed animals playing games of skill and chance, which I ended up leaving behind in the hotel room, because how many stuffed monkeys do you need.

When we left for the airport I casually mentioned, "Maybe the maids will take the stuffed animals home." He never forgave me for that. I'm surprised it didn't make his book. When we met, we were both new to the entertainment business with dreams of becoming writers. We just had no idea how to achieve that dream. Nobody really does when they first get to L.A. You read books, you call annoyed friends of friends to ask about the business, but until you're here, you have no real idea what you're getting into. We both had a string of assistant jobs and questioned whether we would ever make it. We saved our money for nice dinners on birthdays and anniversaries. Our favorite restaurant was Olive Garden. It was our thing.

There was an Olive Garden in Westwood, upstairs in a bank building. You'd never in a million years be able to tell it was there. The only marker visible from the street was a small neon sign in the window. We went there almost every Sunday night, usually after one of his baseball games. We'd wait in line with our square beeper that would light up magically and vibrate when they were ready to serve us food that we would later work off at the gym. In my case I'm still working it off at the gym.

At this Olive Garden, you waited downstairs and when your beeper went off, you hiked up the red carpet staircase to the hostess at the top, who'd show you to your table. We'd ease into large leather rolling chairs or into burgundy leather booths that housed large too-high tables you could barely talk over. Los Angeles doesn't have seasons but the Olive Garden did. It was directly across from the UCLA campus. And we could tell the time of year by the crowd. Fall, start of classes, there would be a lot of eager freshman in there with their nervous parents. Winter Break, you'd see a few foreign kids who hadn't gone home. January would bring groups of friends reunited post-holidays. May was reserved for graduation celebrations. The summer was ours, never a wait. Every season was the same for us, we'd eat endless amounts of "Italian" food and talk about how much we dreaded the upcoming week and how we couldn't believe how long it had been since college. The first time Kyle suggested we go to the

Olive Garden I said I didn't like it. I had zero interest. He pleaded with me to go. It's funny what you do for love. You would never catch me dead there now.

Kyle and I spent time with each other's families. We became best friends and each other's biggest fans. I never doubted he would make it in Hollywood and he never doubted I would. But then doors started to open for me first, and I don't know if we ever came back from that. Our relationship was like an old T-shirt that you love so much you wear it until it gets holes in it. The holes started, and then they just got too big to repair.

When we first started dating, I didn't know anything about dating a guy (well, a straight guy anyway). One night we came home and my cat Emmett had thrown up on the floor. I said, "I'll pick it up later. It's easier to clean when it's dry." He told me he almost walked out the door right then. I don't blame him! What the fuck was I thinking? And my cat Emmett peed in the shower every day, and I would have to clean it out before we got in the next morning. I spent a small fortune on Mr. Clean.

So, I made some rookie mistakes. But for the first time I had a witness to the inner-workings of my life. And together we discovered what it really means to get to know someone. Sharing a bed. Burps. Stomach flus. Farting. Periods. Yeast infections. Bad moods. Poos. Eating aversions (me, sushi; him, anything considered natural in flavor). Boogers. Pimples. Diarrhea. Nipple hair. Loud breathing. All the bad stuff is just out in the open. It has to be because if you spend enough time with someone you can't hide anything.

There were things I loved too. Waking up with someone everyday. Feeling an earthquake in the night and having someone to turn to other than your cats. Having someone to take you to the mechanic.

The airport. Your birthday party. The sweet look on a person's face when they are peacefully asleep and dreaming. The way someone climbs into bed and curls their body up to yours even if they have cold toes. The look on a guy's face when he truly finds something special in you, something you didn't even realize you had.

Kyle liked to get me prizes. If he was out of town and saw something or if he ran to the supermarket without me, he'd come back with some sort of little prize (stomach flu = Barrel of Monkeys).

Kyle was also open to anything. One day we went to a sex shop, which was just a few dusty shelves filled with sex toys in dusty boxes. I bought some leopard print fabric restraints for the wrists and ankles and we were out of there. At home, I was anxious to use them. I got Kyle all hooked up and we "did it." Kyle said, still tied up, "So, that's all it is?"

I nodded my head, "I think so."

Those cuffs made a brief appearance in Kyle's book and now occupy space in a box that sits over my washer and dryer labeled, "Kyle Box. Do not open."

There were so many firsts with Kyle. So many real—and what felt like true—moments that I had never experienced before. I'd always been with the kind of guys who I knew were going to leave me and they did. I would bend and twist myself around them just so I could hold on for dear life but they would always wiggle free. For the first time, I didn't have to cling and he wasn't wiggling. We really wanted and needed each other, two Texas kids floating around the big city, lost until we found each other. Turns out it was mostly a lie. But, at least for a short while, it was a beautiful one.

THE COITAL LAUGH

The first time I called Kyle my boyfriend, I almost cried. We spent the weekend in each others' arms and then when I realized I'd forgotten to take my birth control pills two days in a row, he held me in the bath and said if I was pregnant we'd keep it. We'd raise "it." And our lives would be determined. What a boyfriend I thought I had. Never before in my life had I really been able to use the word boyfriend. Because most of the guys I dated didn't call me their girlfriend I felt like I had waited all my life for someone to notice me and finally he had. Kyle was funny. I was funny. We were funny together. My friends called it the "Kyle & Hilary show." I felt unstoppable with him. Like I could and would make any of my dreams come true. I could write. I could write for a living. I could make it. But that feeling didn't last or it was never real, one of the two.

The first time I told Kyle I loved him, we were in the shower I had just cleaned Emmett's urine out of. We were trading off being in the cold spot where you didn't get as much of the stream. Fog began clouding up the cheap sliding door.

I got kind of quiet and then said loud enough for Kyle to hear over the hard water, "Guess what?"

He said, "What?"

"I love you."

Pause. "Thank you."

He hugged me, politely. It was humiliating. We stood there in the shower hugging, water spilling down my face, washing left-over shampoo into my eyes but that's not what caused the stinging. I was hurt and furious and vulnerable and in love for only the second time in my life with someone who was in "thank you" with me. And he later used this exact dialogue in a viral video advertising his book.

Not too long after that it was Valentine's Day, a day dreaded by singles and those in fledgling relationships. I wrote an incredibly sweet and heartfelt card to Kyle and made him dinner (cornbread casserole, mac-and-cheese, mashed potatoes, salad—I was a carb-addicted vegetarian). He sent me red roses, which I hate, but still appreciated. No guy had ever sent me flowers before. It was embarrassing for some reason, getting them at work and then the card said, "Your Friend, Kyle." I wondered if he specifically told the florist, "Make sure whatever it says, it doesn't say love!" I was a little hurt but I had confidence that he had come around. I was expecting him to tell me that he loved me too over the comforting dinner I'd cooked. The mood was set, the misshaped candles I'd made one Christmas vacation were lit. It was my turn to open my card. I still have it (yes, I save everything).

It was an African American focused Mahogany greeting card with the profile of a girl's curvy body on it. Now remember, I had just given him a super sweet, thoughtful card that clearly expressed how much he meant to me and how much I loved him even though he hadn't told me he was in love with me.

This card, however, had Hallmark crafted sentiment on the front with, "You're stronger, braver, wiser than you've ever been before. Too fine to be defined . . . and too dynamic to ignore. Sexy, graceful, classy- Baby, you're all that and more . . ."

Okay. A little "urban flair." Then I opened it and read what Kyle wrote:

Girl,
Yo' ass gitz betta lookin' every year.
Here's to yo fine ass gittin' mo ripe.
Word.

I had waited months for this. I'd spent a lot of time carefully crafting my card, my words, my feelings. I was furious. He wrote a Valentine's Day card to my ass! I felt the color in my face rise from pink to red. My throat got dry. My eyes itched. It's what I imagine anaphylactic shock is like.

There was only one thing I could get to come out of my mouth, "What?"

Kyle was surprised that I wasn't rolling on the ground laughing. He thought for sure this was a brilliant, hysterical showcase of what a gifted boyfriend I'd chosen. He mistook my anger for an act. He tried to hug me and I wouldn't let him. I wouldn't look him in the eye but I began to rant.

I ranted quickly without many breaths, "I wrote you a thoughtful card. I'm humiliated. All my friends told me, 'He's going to tell you he loves you.' What am I supposed to tell them? If I tell them about this they would hate you."

I stayed up cleaning my apartment because I was too angry to do anything else. Kyle watched not knowing what was going to happen next, he'd certainly never seen me do that before. Every dish was cleaned. The floor sparkled. It hadn't been in better shape since one of my gay ex-boyfriends stayed up all night cleaning, distraught over the death of JFK Jr. In the wee hours of the morning Kyle managed to get back into my good graces. He had a charming way about him. A sweet smile. A hug that made you feel like he was going to take care of you. He reassured me that he was "falling in love" but just wasn't there yet. I accepted this. He knew he screwed up. We decided that for all future birthdays/anniversaries/holidays we would have two cards. A joke one and a real one. And a few months later my patience paid off . . . sort of.

Kyle had gone away on a weekend trip. We'd barely been separated since we started dating. He called me every day. It was clear he missed me. His friends made fun of him for spending the whole trip getting drunk and talking about me and telling them how lucky he was. He told them I was the funniest girl he'd ever met. The night he got back he was so excited to see me. We snuggled in his jersey cotton sheets in his bedroom with large French doors in an apartment filled with nosey roommates and loud UCLA student neighbors. Kyle couldn't stop smiling that sweet smile. He kissed me softly. He touched me like he'd been away for a month not a weekend. Quickly, with enthusiasm, he told me how much he missed me. He told me he didn't want to go away. He didn't have fun without me. He told me that Thundercloud Subs in Austin had the best sandwiches in America. He was just spewing stuff out. He was a million miles away from the guy who wrote a Valentine's Day card to my ass. He told me that he realized over the weekend that he loved me. I didn't say it back right away. In fact, I hadn't said it since that day in the shower, just written it in that Valentine's Day card.

We had sex for the first time as two people in love with each other. He was the first guy to love me back; I'd finally earned the right to listen to love songs. Love is a many splendored thing. Love is exciting and new. All you need *is* love. Finally for me, this wasn't unrequited love, like I had with my backyard trailer living first boyfriend. This was a place you didn't get to with many people. And in retrospect I didn't get there with him, but I thought I did. And maybe he did too. He just didn't know any better then.

And I haven't been in love with anyone since this moment. I've lied about it (used it in a break-up speech as a parting gift once), but I've only experienced a moment like this once in my life. So we celebrated the event with sex. Good sex. I was having sex with someone I loved and who loved me.

When Kyle finished I was hoping he would hold me, but instead he broke out into an uncontrollable, hysterical fit of laughter. Roaring laughter you usually only find around a bunch of people smoking pot. In between laughs, Kyle said he couldn't help it and he couldn't stop himself. He laughed so hard he clutched his stomach and released huge guttural noises that sounded like he'd been saving laughs up for his entire life for this very night.

I was angry. I pushed Kyle off of me. I asked if it was a joke. I doubted everything that had just happened. Did he really even love me? I felt like Carrie covered in a bucket of pig's blood. I felt betrayed. He said it had never happened to him before. It was weird. He said he couldn't control it. Couldn't help it. Couldn't stop it. It went on for a while. Like he'd heard the funniest joke of his life but couldn't remember it to tell me. Which made it even more annoying. I couldn't understand. I couldn't agree, "Oh, that *is* funny." I sat with the navy blue bed-in-a-bag comforter he got for college, pulled up around me with a sour expression. I didn't know if I believed he couldn't control it. It ruined the moment to say the least, my moment in the love spotlight. His laugh had betrayed a deep down truth that night, which I wouldn't learn for years but that you can now buy on a book display at Urban Outfitters.

HAVE YOU BEEN FIGHTING IN FRONT OF THE CAT?

Kyle was the first guy I ever really lived with, other than my cheap gay ex-boyfriend, who was just using me for cable. Kyle and I moved in together because we were in love. We moved to Westwood near UCLA and college students we both felt better than and were jealous of. And with that move, Kyle became the official stepfather to my cats. Emmett and Lolly finally had a daddy.

Emmett is a wonderful cat; liked by cat lovers and non-cat lovers alike. But he's a bad cat. He likes to bite. He likes to claw. He likes to scratch delicate human skin on hands and faces. He also likes to pee anywhere but in his litter box. In our new place it was the dining room, even though Emmett and Lolly had an entire bathroom of their own. This apparently wasn't good enough for him; he was a free pee-er. He couldn't be boxed in to do his business. Like a dad who pees in his front yard because he can, that's just Emmett.

One night I heard Emmett crying. I ran down the concrete staircase and he was sitting in the living room with a pained look on his face, trying to pee but only a tiny watery bloody drop came out. I freaked out. I feared first for Emmett and then for myself, because when you are making a couple hundred bucks a week, pet emergencies aren't in the budget. I yelled out to Kyle and we were off to the twenty-four-hour emergency holistic new-age-y vet (this *is* California after all). He was reluctant to leave his computer but he knew it was one of his boyfriend duties and that shirking it would surely lead to a night without sex.

Emmett was in with the vet for a while. They did a bunch of tests and x-rays. When we were finally allowed in for the consultation with the vet, a tall blonde guy with hair that sat on his head like a Muppet, and who seemed not to care about shaving, he looked over his notes while Kyle and I anxiously waited for him to speak. Then finally he sighed and said, "So, there is blood in Emmett's urine. And he seems to be having trouble peeing."

Tell us something we don't know, I thought.

He continued, "We can't find a medical reason for why this is happening." Pause. "Do you guys fight a lot?"

Kyle and I turned to each other. I felt like we were in the emergency room, claiming our kid broke his arm falling down the stairs. And that he hit his eye on the doorknob.

I couldn't lie, "We do fight a lot. Bicker mostly. Not major stuff."

Kyle nodded. It's true. We did bicker about things like whose turn was it to buy shower gel, and if you did buy shower gel, why did you buy the man smell one which is way too beach-y and Old Spice-y for me and smells like guys balls when they're trying to score with a girl. Why didn't you get the kind of toilet paper we usually buy? I asked for *Diet* Coke. We'd fight about Kyle putting away his laundry and about eating healthy. For a while Kyle refused to eat dinner because he thought he was fat. I called him anorexic. But really I was jealous of the discipline. We'd fight over whether or not it was okay to kill a spider that had found its way into the house. He felt like it wasn't okay, karma. I felt like they were trespassing, karma. We fought over his wardrobe. I was sick of his "Jesus Pieces" shirt, which he wore ironically. He thought I looked overweight in skirts. We fought about his buddies. One of whom I got into a huge fight with because he thought AIDS in Africa was a ruse.

The vet didn't know the half of it. I guess we fought about everything. And yes, we did do it in front of the cats.

The vet thought for a minute, "I think your fighting is causing Emmett to be stressed out and that's why he's having trouble passing urine."

Kyle looked confused. "We're making Emmett pee blood?"

"Yes," the vet said, completely sure of his diagnosis.

I felt like shit. I knew fighting stressed me out but I had no idea it was stressing Emmett out too.

The vet offered this advice: "Just try not to raise your voices around him for a while. Cats are very sensitive."

The next few days, Emmett continued to have problems. Kyle and I continued to have problems too but made an effort not to raise our voices. But one night, things got out of hand. I have no idea what we were arguing about but it was definitely heated. We were standing in the living room yelling over the couch at each other, while Emmett sat on the sofa's arm in between us. At one point when Kyle and I were both talking loudly/yelling/I was yelling; Emmett meowed aggressively and put his paw up the air. Now, I realize this sounds like total bullshit and if someone was telling me this, I wouldn't believe it, but it happened—ask Kyle (or look for it in his next book). Emmett stopped us dead in our tracks; his little paw raised as if to say, "Just stop it already." His meow was intense and commanding. We both looked at the cat. Then we looked at each other. We started laughing which immediately turned to crying for me. We *were* making Emmett pee blood. The stress of our relationship was too much for him to take. And if it was too much for him to take, then what was it doing to us?

A few days later, Emmett was worse and I took him to a different vet. Turns out he had crystals in his urine that were blocking his urethra. It was more about diet than emotion. The new vet laughed when I told her about the shaggy headed holistic vet that would have put us in couples' therapy before he'd have put a catheter in Emmett, which is what he really needed. But if there'd also been a catheter for our relationship I wouldn't have turned it down.

A QUESTIONABLE POO:
THE END OF ROMANCE

When I imagined living with a guy, it meant eating breakfast in bed and painting the bedroom walls lime green because we could! But that wasn't the reality. I spent a lot of time writing, which really meant watching *Road Rules* marathons, and Kyle spent most of his time playing video games (he had almost every console ever sold and we had a Street Fighter II arcade game in our living room). For a while, his drug of choice was an online computer game set in the *Star Wars* universe. One afternoon after logging about four hours of play, I asked if we could please go to Olive Garden. I always started asking about an hour before I really wanted to go. Kyle said he couldn't go for a while because he had to wait in a line to buy a ticket for the shuttle to planet Tatooine or something like that. He missed the shuttle, which was "total bullshit" apparently. I used to listen to hours of video game talk. A lot of it involved Kyle talking about how awesome he was at them. Halo? Can't touch him. Street Fighter I & II? Don't even try. Final Fantasy? Destroyed every single one. *Star Wars* Galaxies? Couldn't hold his attention—yawn. He saved the princess in Super Mario Bros. before he was born!

While Kyle raged about missing the shuttle, I said something like "Can't you just take the later shuttle?" This showed that I clearly didn't "get the game" and it upset him. He wanted to put his head through "the fucking wall." I was about to try to get him to explain, like a good girlfriend, when all of a sudden something was not right.

My *stomach* was not right. Not right at all. I hurried to the bathroom and . . . BOOM. Without a premonition ("I had the weirdest dream . . .") or a Soothsayer to warn me ("Thou will encounter a disastrous natural occurrence."), there it was . . . a questionable poo. Nothing normal about it. It looked like I shit out an alien shitting out an alien. My mind instantly jumped to colon/rectal/anal cancer. Then I thought intestinal cancer/colostomy bag. Then I thought I might immediately be on death's doorstep. I dropped to my knees. I didn't flush. How could I flush? I thought it might have been the equivalent of a suicide note. The medical examiner would enter our semi-clean bathroom and find me on the mostly dirty Orange Julius colored bathmat. Dead. He would look in the toilet and say, "Oh, there you go. Cause of death: a questionable poo." I moved myself onto the cold aquamarine tile floor for a few minutes and leaned against our beloved tub.

From the other room Kyle yelled, "What are you doing in there?"

Like a kid covered in crumbs trying to deny their use of the cookie jar, I yelled back, "Nothing."

I stared a while longer at the poo. It stared back at me. Sometimes a poo is an accomplishment. When it's long. Complete. Unbowed and unbroken. That's the kind of poo when a parent awards a potty-training child with a Skittle. This was not the case. I looked angrily at my stomach like it might give me some answers. Then I gathered my courage and walked into the other room. I sat at my desk, swiveled in my faux leather chair for a second, silent.

Kyle finally stopped typing and noticed I was paler-faced and quiet. "What's wrong with you?"

Without making eye contact, I said, "I need to show you something."

His eyes found mine. I nodded.

I took a deep breath and then closed my eyes, "I need to show you my poo."

Kyle reacted violently and quickly, "No! What?"

I tried to explain, "It's questionable. I need you to go look at it. I would never ask you if it wasn't an emergency. Don't make this harder than it is."

Kyle looked at me knowing he had no argument. This is what a boyfriend of four-plus years does. This *was* an emergency. This was love. It may not be the lyrics of a hit song, but it could be. "Love love me poo . . ." Kyle left his avatar alone in the galaxy, probably walking in place against the corner of a virtual house he designed. A house he spent more time on than our own. Kyle walked into the bathroom. I waited at my desk, still in shock. From the other room, I heard some dramatic exclamations. He re-entered, visibly upset.

"That's not right." He didn't make eye contact.

Scared, I barely got out, "What do you think it is?"

He speculated. Cancer? Worms? Butt boogers? I asked questions neither of us could answer. At least I had a witness. Someone who could speak to a doctor or at my funeral or to the press. Whichever was necessary.

After a minute, Kyle told me to flush it. He wanted me to have the last look. I did. I hoped out-loud it was nothing and hoped secretly it was a tapeworm that would get me to my high school weight.

I returned to my computer; Kyle returned to waiting for his shuttle. We sat quietly while I scoured medical websites that do nothing to alleviate fears. In fact they arm you with information to create new fears. As we sat in silence in the office we shared. In the home we shared. I felt it. After almost five years, the romance had have officially ended. We were roommates. Buddies. Friends. Not lovers. Not anymore.

WITCHES BOARDING SCHOOL: MY SEXUAL FANTASY

Kyle was obsessed with 69. He wanted to do it every time we had sex, which for someone who isn't a small chick becomes humiliating at some point. It's funny though for as much as he bashed my ass in print he seemed to want to see a lot of it from that vantage point. I often felt like I was involved in a sex act with Kyle versus just having sex. It was always about the destination and never about the journey. Maybe this is why he loved talking about sex robots. He was fascinated with what would happen when robots could perform as perfect sexual partners. He believed it would be the end of marriage as we know it. I should have been concerned with the hope in his voice during these discussions.

I was not a sex robot, unfortunately for Kyle, and I think it was because his process was labor intensive. Not only did it start with 69 it also started with a bath. I believe Kyle had OCD (Obsessive Compulsive Disorder). Now he doesn't think this is true but it's pretty undeniable in my opinion. Evidence:

1) He signs all his money and refuses to part with it until he has signed it. I waited often at counters of stores for this process to take place.

2) He had to take baths all the time. The idea of getting into bed without taking a shower wasn't just disgusting to him but disturbing. I have never taken more baths than when we dated. Even the gay guys didn't take baths.

3) Kyle liked being naked because clothing restricted him.

4) Kyle liked food that was in meal-sized portions. He came close to flat out refusing to eat food that had been prepared in our home unless it was leftovers from Olive Garden. He wanted to be able to have a unit of food and not decipher that unit on his own. He also liked eating Subway every day so he could predict his shits.

5) Kyle always left one bite of food over after every meal. He called this his "Sacrifice to the Gods of Chaos." Not that he really believed in any gods, it was just his way of describing the action and justifying the need to do this action. Even if he ate a mini-Snickers bar he would throw out half. If he didn't, something horrible would happen, obviously.

These things may sound innocent to you, but they dictated our life and I didn't realize how much until we parted ways. Until I had sex with someone after a night out because we were ready to have sex and not just because we just finished our ritual cleansing. Kyle's peccadilloes finally took a toll on our relationship.

Kyle and I used to have sex every day but towards the end it was more like every other day. This bugged him. He told me his friend at work had sex three times a day with his ex-lesbian girlfriend. I told him his friend was a liar. He thought we should be having sex more often and I didn't know how that was possible. He used to complain that I didn't meet him at the door when he got home from work naked or just wearing Saran wrap. When he told me that, it made me feel like just me being there when he got home from work wasn't enough.

Sometimes when Kyle and I had sex I felt like we were sixteen and fooling around in the back of a car. Not in an exciting way but in a, "Wow, can you believe we're doing this" way. And I could believe we were doing it. We were adults. Adults who lived together. I wanted sex to be, for lack of a better word, serious.

It was this desire for sincerity or drama that made my mind start to wander. I didn't think about celebrities or old flames, it was way more specific than that. I was a witch. A teenage witch, attending boarding school for witches. I was with a warlock and we were having sex in the locker room where the students keep their flying broom-sticks. When I was on top it was always the same. It was fall. There was a "first day of school" excitement in the air. Witches were at the school bookstore stocking up on supplies and we were sneaking off for SEX. I had a pointy hat and a high GPA. Pretending to be a witch was the only way I could finish. I don't know where it came from but I was happy to have it. But sadly, it meant just thinking about Kyle wasn't enough. I had to 69 with a warlock.

THE SADDEST BATH

The cracks in my relationship with Kyle grew larger and larger with each anniversary and its accompanying impersonal electronics gift. First went our sex. Then went our trust. Then our friendship. Finally, we were just roommates who rolled their eyes a lot.

Kyle and I broke up on a hot, sticky August night in 2004. And we still slept in bed together, but for the first time platonically. It was easily eighty degrees outside and ninety degrees inside. The heat of the day was trapped in our A/C-less house. Our velvet, quilted comforter was folded at our feet. I'd gotten it for Christmas from my parents, despite their knowledge that it would be used by two people living in sin.

When I told my dad we were moving in together, he said, "Oh my God. Absolutely not. What are we going to tell your grandmother?"

I responded by saying, "We're going to get married. Don't worry about it."

Kyle and I held each other, uncertain of the future. We both cried ourselves to sleep against each other's familiar warmth. It's amazing that the body can even sleep at times like that. I'd been gone from that bed for a month when it all went down.

Kyle picked me up at the airport. I'd just come back from New York. Almost the entire month of August I was helping my sister move to New York, her first foray out of Texas. Kyle didn't come and visit me while I was there. The moment I saw him, his outgrown blonde hair, hunched over stance, and his uniform black T-shirt and Nike shoes someone might beat him up to steal, I knew something was drastically different. I could tell he was dreading my arrival.

I got to baggage claim and we hugged. Lovers do not hug at airports. Lovers who haven't seen each other in a month don't hug, they kiss. I knew.

During the embrace I kind of mumbled, "So good to see you."

That's what you say when you run into a former coworker at the movies, not what you say to the man you love. There were no flowers like the last time he picked me up at the airport, because he knew there was going to be no sex. Conversation was forced and there was a wall that had not been there when I left.

Looking to fill the silence I said, "So, how are the cats?"

"Fine, you need to clean the litter box," he said coldly.

"Are you feeling sick?"

"No. Yeah, maybe a little."

It was clear he wasn't interested in celebrating my return. We stopped at the In-N-Out Burger drive-thru because I was starving. Kyle said he wasn't hungry. He let me pay, which wasn't typical either. We went home.

After scarfing down a burger, I started going through my mail and blathering on about the trip and my sister and her Lab, Guthrie, and the Direct TV on the plane and how Jet Blue is a pretty cool airline and other stupid things I wouldn't have said if I knew he was about to break up with me. I would have used our last conversation to cover something more resonant. Why did you fall in love with me? What makes me special? Do you think I'm a good writer?

I also took my shirt off, unbuttoning each button of my long-sleeve pink Polo.

Posing with hands on hips, I said, "Guess who lost weight with all the walking in New York?"

It was an attempt to lure him out of his bad mood and frosty demeanor. That was the second to the last time he would see me naked. He barely looked at me and I felt like I did in fourth grade when I found out Eddie Ledbetter didn't like me back. It seemed to take a lot longer to button the shirt back up. And to tell you the truth I was hoping I wouldn't have to.

Neither of us mentioned the tension. We went upstairs to our bedroom and I began unpacking my rag-tag discount store luggage. He sat on the bed, a mess of cat-hair and souvenirs from New York. I handed him the last present I would ever give him. A sleeveless black shirt with an iron-on baboon that said "Bronx Zoo," in '80s graffiti font. He thanked me in a way that made me feel stupid for buying it.

After a few minutes I couldn't take it anymore, "So, is there something going on?"

Kyle pet a snoring Emmett as his voice shook a little bit, "While you were gone I was trying to decide if I wanted to propose when you got back or break up."

I shot back quickly, "I'm guessing you're not proposing." With bitch emphasis on *proposing.*

Kyle gathered his confidence. "I've decided that I don't want to get married, don't want to have kids, and I am going to cryogenically freeze myself. I've already started the paperwork."

Kyle was telling me he didn't want to be with me AND that he wanted to live forever. Essentially he was saying I want to live for eternity without *you.* I'd sensed on the phone that he was pulling away. It wasn't the cell reception like he claimed. It was that every time my name came up on his phone, his heart sank and broke all at the same time because he knew what he was going to do to me. Maybe if I wanted to save it, I should have come running home.

I am witty and dramatic when self-righteous.

Trying to sting hard, I said something very close to, "I can't wait to fuck other people. I'm going to go fuck an older, *successful* writer."

As soon as Kyle started the break up, I began to sort our old college textbooks, mismatched kitchenware, unread scripts, dirty laundry, liquor bottles, towels, and tiny travel-sized shampoos. I grabbed my just-unpacked suitcases and began cleaning out the closets. He followed me around, confused, afraid. I kept telling him this was the reality and that I should be smart and get a start on packing, no time like the present. Maybe he should too. This is what it meant to break up; you split everything apart. I wanted him to see the consequences of his actions. The consequence of that decision he made alone over a summer in our hotbox of a townhouse, while he sat in rooms filled with pictures of us happy together (like the ones from his parents' backyard that would later be posted on his sister's Facebook page with me cropped out), among things we had bought each other (his and her robot portraits), petting cats we'd created nicknames for together (Korfaleque and Biggest Boy). To drive home my point, my anger, my lesson, I got on craigslist and started looking for apartments—singles apartments. We were only thirty minutes into our break-up.

I angrily spat, "This is what happens when people break up. You are never going to see me again."

Kyle watched from the bed, on sheets that I was sure hadn't been changed since I left.

He sighed and said cautiously, "I think you want things that I can't give you."

I furiously stuffed my trunk that I'd had since going to "Heart of the Hills" sleep-away camp in junior high. "No, it's just that you can't give them to me right now. You're going to get married and have kids, eventually, it'll just be with someone else."

I saw "the look" on his face, the look of someone taking you from the A list to the D list. The look of someone who will still remember your phone number a year later but never dial it. It was too much for me to take, the idea that Kyle has clearly prepared for this. I asked if there was somebody else, some slut who had clearly violated the girl code of ethics. He said no. I didn't believe it but at this point I wouldn't have believed anything he said.

Kyle and I had taken a bath together almost every morning we'd been together. Almost five years of baths. The morning after we broke up, I had a job interview and Kyle had work, which he often referred to as "shoveling shit." He got up first and ran the bath. The start of the bath and its temperature was always his responsibility. Sometimes it was too hot because he liked to "burn the stink off." He got in the water and then I came into the bathroom. I took off my still-wet-from-tears nightclothes off. He was surprised but he didn't stop me.

Stepping into the water I commented, "It's hot."

And those were all the words we spoke, while we sat toboggan style in our long '30s-era tub surrounded by almost-never-cleaned tile. I would like to say I got into the tub because it was routine and it was what I knew. But I got into that tub because I needed him to feel me. I needed him to know I was there, that I existed, that I was in pain, that I was not going to vanish and make this easier for him.

When we were first looking at the apartment, the building manager offered as a selling point that there was a little rise above the tub perfect for resting a bottle of wine. There had never been, and would never be a bottle of wine there.

I stared at Kyle's smooth, freckled back as he poured water over it from a cup I got from Spring Fling in college. I traced the ugly tattoo of a dragon he had on his right shoulder blade. He'd drawn it himself and gotten it when he turned eighteen. It was hideous, but in a way I would miss it. I looked at my fat, pale and lumpy thighs under the now soapy water. The night before I'd been proud they looked slimmer, but they were huge. They were the thighs of a woman who gets left by her boyfriend. Kyle turned around to offer me the musky smelling man body wash I'd always ask him not to buy, and for the first time I felt naked in front of him. We bathed in silence. And of all the hundreds if not thousands of baths we took together, this was the saddest.

MY LANDING STRIP
IS STUCK TO YOU

In the days after Kyle and I broke up, I was vicious. My punishment was cruel and unusual. I laid out in detail how I was going to go have sex with guys who were hotter than him, had more money, knew more about wine, were taller, and had smaller foreheads. I knew which buttons to push and he felt too guilty to fight back. After two nights in our bedroom, on our full bed that had never seemed smaller, Kyle moved onto the couch. The micro-fiber, faux-suede couch in espresso brown from Crate and Barrel. More specifically MY couch that he refused to help pay for.

I couldn't sleep. At night I would sit up in bed hyperventilating and reliving every second of our lives together. I kept remembering something I hadn't thought about. The upcoming trip I had planned to visit his family! Our joint phone number! My ovaries shriveling up like Shrinky Dinks! I'd saved every card and gift big and small (DVD player, tumbled rocks from a Western restaurant in Dallas) that he had ever given me, and everything that would fit in a box I put on Kyle's desk chair (the crappiest ugliest chair on the planet that had tennis balls stuck on the legs). At choice moments, I would pull from the box of pain like a Bingo caller pulling a number and read a card aloud, shouting to wherever he was in the house, "Remember when you wrote, 'You are the most amazing girl I have ever met?'

Remember when you couldn't imagine spending a night without me? Remember when you went on a trip to Austin to visit your friends and realized you were in love with me and couldn't wait to get back!? I hate you, you selfish mother-fucker!"

A few days after the break-up, I was back looking on craigslist for an apartment. I found an ad that read:

"Do you like beer, hot bitches, and video games? Do want to live in a mansion?"

The ad disgusted me. Who did this guy think he was? What a fucking pig. What kind of "hot bitch" would sleep with this loser? And then I saw the e-mail address. This guy was Kyle. Of course it was.

Three days ago he was thinking about proposing to me and now he's looking to live in a mansion with a bunch of dudes who drink beer and fuck hot chicks.

I read the ad several times before the anger traveled to my fingertips and I forwarded it to my closest friends and his mom, with the subject heading: "Why is he doing this to me?!"

I called him at work and chewed him out. He had some lame excuse that I couldn't even hear through my rage. I told him his writing was going to have to be better than that ad if he wanted to make it out here. And I would know because I was actually a WORKING writer. I'd been with him for almost five years, and in an instant he'd become a stranger. Not just a stranger. A fucking loser, asshole stranger, who wanted to drink beer and fuck sluts, and live with a bunch of dudes. Who has roommates at 28?!

I had to do something. Something confident. Something strong. Something classy but that would still quench my thirst for revenge. I brought it to my Ladies Poker Group. I knew they would help. I've never met a more wonderful group of women. Supportive (they will take a cookie out of your mouth if you are trying to lose weight), understanding (they let you go home with that guy who's bad for you because you want to), brutally honest (the next day they tell you that you aren't allowed to ever see that guy again), and open (to the point of describing anal sex in so much detail I won't ever be having it).

They all agreed on what I needed to do. They all agreed that the road to being a confident, independent woman went through Vladka.

Vladka was born in the Czech Republic when it wasn't the Czech Republic and is in her fifties. She is cold and hard and matter-of-fact. She is a waxer.

Since I was not used to letting people examine my vulva without an MD behind their name, I was nervous. Vladka's office was in the back of a Vietnamese nail salon, which was full of neon colors and bad décor choices. There was a lot of yelling by Vietnamese women in Spandex and when I asked, a younger woman politely told me in English that I was in the right place. Then Vladka finally emerged, waving me inside with a brisk, "Come on." A woman with oversized sunglasses and an expensive handbag pushed past me on her way out. If I hadn't known better, I would have been convinced Vladka was selling knock-off Gucci bags or coke back there. Vladka introduced herself in firm but accented English.

After standing there for a few seconds, she said, "Okay, now why you aren't getting undressed?"

With that demand I got out of my clothes and on the white paper covered table. I told her I was in the Ladies Poker Group. I told her, "I've never done this before," like a virgin whispering to her high school boyfriend.

Vladka barely moved a mouth muscle, "I have heard of this group. I do all the girls."

She began pouring baby powder all over my lady spot. I could feel myself sweating. I didn't know you could sweat down there. Well, not that much.

I instantly made excuses for myself, "I think I'm a little sweaty."

Vladka softened. "Nothing to be nervous of."

I stayed nervous and got chatty, "My boyfriend and I just broke up."

Vladka found her groove. "Good for you. I'm too tired for men. Makes life complicated."

She was right. My life was much more complicated. I told her our story and why we were breaking up. He doesn't want kids. Doesn't want to get married. Wants to freeze himself for all eternity so he can screw sex robots. She told me he was a child. It meant so much coming from her, even though she was a stranger. She made me feel like this was a universal problem. Kyle was everyone's problem. It wasn't me. She prepared the first wax strip and ripped.

I had been lulled into a false sense of security, "Eghhhhh!"

Vladka, knowing she tricked me, announced, "It's better if I don't tell you it is coming."

That was exactly what Kyle had done.

I picked myself mentally off the floor. I could take this. "I just was surprised."

Vladka began to tell me her life story, as she continued to rip surprised pubic hair out of me with hot wax. The process was both soothing and excruciatingly painful. The end result was . . . red. But it was almost entirely hairless. I'd seen my anatomy in a new light, figuratively and literally under the bright fluorescent bulbs of the back room at the Vietnamese nail salon.

Vladka, proud of her work, said, "Looks good, no?"

She was right to be proud. Because I felt transformed. As she wiped me down with some more baby powder, I felt beautiful. I felt sexy. I felt something I hadn't felt ever.

"Vladka, my landing strip is stuck to you."

I got unstuck and went "home," though it didn't feel like a much of a home at that point. It was more like a war zone. If it were *Different Strokes* or *Growing Pains*, we would have put masking tape down the center of the apartment. I walked in the door to find Kyle playing video games, of course. Naked, of course. In MY chair, of course.

I set the cheese in the trap. "Guess what?"

Kyle looked up, wearing an X-box Live headset, "What?"

He paused the video game and I'm sure he thought I had another rant or apology or plea bargain.

"I just got a Brazilian wax and somebody else is going to get to use it."

Kyle acted like he didn't care. We were caught up in the fight. It's what gets you through the break-up initially but it doesn't keep you from having emotional flashbacks. I saw one cross his face. We did love each other. And the one thing that wasn't going to be in his mansion filled with beer, video games, and hot bitches; was me.

And for the first time since he uttered the words, "I'm cryogenically freezing myself," I felt like maybe, just maybe, I was going to be okay.

———

After a break-up, I like to do a fair evaluation of each party just in case I ever need a reminder of why it went south in the first place:

WHAT IS WRONG WITH HIM
1) Too many baths
2) Eating outside makes him feel like an animal, so no picnics or lovely outdoor cafes
3) Too much nakedness (balls are just plain gross)
4) Too much nakedness on my furniture (balls on furniture are even grosser)
5) Made jokes at my expense ("Have you met my fat pig girlfriend, Hilary?")
6) Doesn't like to travel to places other than the Olive Garden (Exception being ComiCon, which I went to . . . TWICE!)
7) Obsessed with freezing himself, sex robots, regular robots
8) Wrote book about me in which he referred to me as his "fat-assed girlfriend"
9) Made me wait for hours on end while he finished levels in video games ("I just have to find the sniper and then we can go.")
10) Ironic Jesus T-shirts make up half his wardrobe, and the other half are ill-fitting, crotch-hugging shorts
11) Refuses to clean litter box, though enjoyed company of cats
12) Only eats hamburgers, chicken fingers, and steak. Actually likes Big Red, the DRINK.
13) He left me

WHAT IS WRONG WITH ME
1) Like to be alone too much
2) Have two cats including one with diabetes and one who licks all the hair of her belly and genitals (recently the vet called, concerned, to ask me about what was happening in the home environment . . .)
3) Don't eat sushi or Asian food
4) Dislike everyone who is better than me
5) Think everyone is better than me
6) Have toe nail fungus on more than one toe
7) Get angry for no reason (but am really witty when angry)
8) Have bizarre sexual fantasy scenarios which involve witches, academia, and exotic travel
9) Always trying to lose ten pounds (always lie about having to lose ten pounds, when I really need to lose fifteen or twenty)
10) Always feel like I want something but I don't know what it is . . . i.e., perpetually dissatisfied
11) Like to nap a lot
12) Don't know how to cook (except Frito Pie)
13) Let him break up with me
14) Say I like to ski because it sounds cool, but then don't like it that much when I'm doing it
15) Am the type of person who makes a list of things that are wrong with someone

---

PART 4

NO
MORE
BATHS
(WELL, MAYBE
A FEW MORE)

A REAL, GENUINE, 100-PERCENT BONA FIDE CHRISTMAS MIRACLE

A month after Kyle and I broke up, we moved out of our Westwood townhouse, out of our tandem parking spots, and out of each other's lives. We'd lived together for a month after breaking up. We were exhausted. We were done. I was terrified. We met one last night to clean the place. And over a few cleaning products, in a place that felt more empty than when we'd moved in, we said good-bye.

I spent the next few weeks sleeping on a deflated air mattress on the floor of my new itty-bitty apartment and getting rid of the Biblical fly infestation. The owner of the building swore she'd never seen anything like it. And I believed her. I'd brought it all with me. Luckily, flies have a short lifespan.

I was deeply sad. The anger had been depleted and it's all that was left. It was the kind of sad where you stop in the middle of doing something to think about how sad you are. Load of dirty towels in your arms about to put them into the wash. "Was I just not pretty enough? What if I had blue eyes?" Boiling water, spilling out and sizzling on the Hotpoint budget cook top. "There probably *was* another girl." A skinnier girl. A girl with real red hair. Opening a can of cat food, with cats purring and rubbing holes in your jeans. "Nobody will ever love me again." In line at the bank, in what could only be considered not-public clothes. "I am unlovable." But with all of that doubt and sadness, never once did I call Kyle. I wanted to punish him and I knew he was in withdrawal too. Why ease his pain?

My new building was technically nice. Built in the '90s by a lover of the '80s, the whole thing was the color of rust and periwinkles with bright Cheerios-yellow accented metal railings. Everything seemed in good working order and clean. But there were the flies and then within the first two weeks my apartment flooded twice . . . from the toilet. It ruined the new furniture I could not afford but bought anyway. The building manager was a black cowboy who constantly watched John Wayne movies and wrote pulp fiction, which he recited on his answering machine: "The busty blonde couldn't fit inside her silk blouse covered in plump red cherries but the detective knew he couldn't look. He knew her brute of a husband was waiting outside dragging off a Cuban cigar and looking for an excuse to put someone six feet under in a Chicago overcoat—BEEP."

I wanted to be alone because I felt alone, and this one-bedroom was an easy place to do it. It was small, dark, and at the back of the building. I rarely saw my neighbors and that's how we all liked it.

After settling in, I entered a period of self-reflection and weight gain. Mimosas, Tylenol PM, burritos, and S'mores—my drugs of choice. And don't think I didn't realize at the time how sad it was to roast marshmallows on a plastic fork over a gas flame in a decorative fireplace. It was hobo-esque, but those were tough times. I was nauseous and the only thing I could think of eating for some reason was marshmallows. Bags of them.

Christmas marked three months of being broken up and it was the first Christmas in a long time I didn't have to pick out a present for Kyle that he would semi-appreciate and stick in a drawer. My birthday, Halloween, Thanksgiving passed and they'd all been a blur. But this was the one holiday I couldn't ignore. I had to go home.

When Kyle and I broke up, I didn't know how to handle it with my parents, who would surely say, "I told you so." I had in fact guaranteed them that we were getting married. I sent them an e-mail a few days after it happened. All it said was something like this:

"Kyle and I broke up. It's very sad. I'm not ready to talk about it. You were right. I need sixteen hundred dollars for a new apartment. Hilary."

I don't think I ever really talked to them about it. It was just understood that I had failed. Now I was living in Hollywood alone with no job and expired LSAT scores.

I had to go home for Christmas. I've never not been with my parents on Christmas, and they *had* sent me sixteen hundred dollars. I went home and hit the Christmas cookies hard. I was surrounded by family and more alone than I'd ever felt in Lost Angeles because I couldn't be honest with them. I had to pretend it was all for the best, even though I didn't know that yet. We sat down to Christmas Eve dinner all wearing brightly colored paper crowns we'd gotten from our Christmas Crackers and I saw something. Something happening outside the window.

I couldn't believe what I was seeing, "It's snowing!"

My mom barely even looked. "It's not snowing. It's rain. Sit down and eat your dinner."

I love that my mom didn't think I knew the difference between rain and snow. I ran to the backyard and stood by our pool to witness something that hadn't happened in Corpus Christi, Texas, in 107 years . . . snow falling. The sky was full of these determined little snowflakes, making their way to the Earth in of all places South Texas. They'd clearly gotten the address wrong. My sister came out and my parents finally followed. My mom was still in denial until she saw the snowflakes fall on her Christmas sweater. It was a miracle. It snowed all night and covered the palm trees and beaches. Thousands of kids and adults, who had never seen snow before in their entire lives, woke up to a white Christmas. A completely totally WHITE CHRIST-MAS. Before that morning, for most people in South Texas, the phrase "White Christmas" had only existed in Christmas songs and in black-and-white holiday movies with unrealistic endings. This snow made anything seem possible. There were snowmen and snow angels and snow castles (it is a beach town). It was a present that made every-one happy, that made everyone feel like a kid on Christmas morning and didn't cost a thing, if you don't count global warming. It was a real, genuine, 100 percent bona fide Christmas miracle.

Not to sound narcissistic but it was clear this was a direct message from the universe to me, personally. I had to re-enter the world again. No more Kyle. No more baths. No more sulking. No more S'mores. I is going to have fun. I was going to leave the apartment. I was going to lose weight. I was going to talk to my neighbors. I was going to get a real bed. I was going to stop calling Tylenol PM and champagne dessert. I was going to date. Not like I dated before, desperate and clinging to every guy I met like I'm being carried away by rising floodwater and looking for anything I can get my hands on. This time I *was* the rising floodwater. My life was moving. And I wanted someone to come along for the ride. I finally saw I deserved that. Certainly the universe was ready to let me have it. Everyone has that moment, where they come out of the darkness. And this was it. These little snowflakes freed me. It's when my real post-Kyle life began. I thought, in a world where mir-acles happen on Christmas Eve, why couldn't one happen to me? What I didn't realize was that the miracle had already happened.

DELTA EMPLOYEE VERSUS A HEARTBROKEN EMOTIONAL EATER

During what turned out to be a fairly long stint of unemployment, A.K. (After Kyle), I decided to go to New York to see my sister. I'd booked a non-stop flight. The seats on the airplane seemed to be smaller than the last time I'd flown. Certainly it wasn't *my* size.

A few hours into the flight, the pilot came over the PA system to say, "Hello, this is the pilot here. Just wanted to let you know we are going to have to make an unscheduled stop in Atlanta."

Atlanta is nowhere near New York. There was no more explanation. The passengers, in unison, entered a sort of silent panic. It was so quiet you could have heard a pen drop or the engine explode. My theory on plane crashes has always been if it happens to me, at least I don't have to do my taxes again (which I don't even do, my dad does them) or wash the dishes. But luckily, we landed in Atlanta without incident. I would live for my dad to see another tax season.

Once off the plane, the Delta employees pointed us toward a customer service desk. After thirty minutes of waiting, we were directed to another desk, which was apparently the customer-waiting desk. By the time I actually got up to the right place, there were no more flights to New York that night. I was stuck in Hotlanta, even though I had a New York/L.A. non-stop ticket. I called my sister to break the news. It wasn't clear if she even remembered I was coming.

I'd never been to Atlanta before, and I thought it could be fun. Determined, I set out to enjoy my night alone in Atlanta. I maintained hope that the motel would have a pool. After getting a new flight assignment for way-too-early the next morning, I was pointed toward yet another line. This was the Space Mountain line of the airport and I didn't have a Fast Pass. My arms were sore from an overloaded carry-on bag that contained nothing I would need for an overnight stay. I regretted checking my luggage. I regretted deciding to even take this trip in the first place. My once positive attitude had taken an ugly turn after hour two of waiting. Then at last, I was at the front. Glory. Glory. Glory.

A handsome dimpled Delta Employee spoke to me in a soft, soothing Barry White voice. I'm sure he was there because he had an aptitude for dealing with potentially angry customers. I also guess he'd slept with a few. He had that kind of charm.

Dimpled dude got off to a great start, "Sorry about the delay." And then it went downhill, "I can't help but notice that you're . . ."

He pantomimed a pregnant belly. My horrified look must have said it all. The female Delta employee next to him looked at him and shook her head and her high ponytail with it. I was in total shock and so was everyone in earshot. We were maybe in shock about different things. Me, that it could be said. Them, that it had been said.

The mood changed, but the employee continued, "I thought I saw a little bump."

I let my low self-esteem hang out, "Well, you did. But it's not a baby." It was a burrito/S'mores belly.

This is when most reasonable, rational-thinking beings would step off. But, no, the guy then came out from around the counter to get a better look.

He tried to defend himself, "See . . . I . . ."

He looked to the other passengers in line for approval. They all looked at the floor. The female employee shook her head and pony-tail again. Now, a certain type of person (i.e. an emotionally healthy individual) would have let this go. Or perhaps told him that it was rude to ask.

I am not a normal person. I told him, "I will have you know that I have been making healthier eating choices and I've been working out with a personal trainer twice a week. Seth! We can call him."

I *had* been working out with a trainer. He was short and feisty and the only thing he loved more than having sex with Asian women was telling me about it. He once dated a transvestite and assured me, "She's all girl from the waist up." When you think about it, is half really enough? And that half?

The airline guy wasn't moved by my workout argument. I wanted him to say something like, "That's great you're working out" or, "It *is* hard to make healthy eating choices. It *is* hard to be a woman in today's society. I see you're from L.A. It must be even harder there." But no, he continued to defend his initial offense. He told me that he only said something because he thought it was terrible that the father of my baby was letting me travel alone. I reminded him I was not having a baby, so he could lay-off judging the non-existent baby's deadbeat dad. The female employee looked at me sympathetically, but never said anything. Her facial expressions and eyebrows alone were bitching the guy out. Maybe if I hadn't been at such a low point in my life, I would have just told him that you don't say that to women ever, just to be safe. I should've schooled him on the right thing to say. But I *was* at a low point. So, I lost it. I told him that I was going to lose the weight, that I had lost a lot of weight in college by becoming a vegetarian and lifting small five-pound weights. I told him I just started and that it took time if you did it right. I told him that I was just out of a long-term relationship with a guy who had devastated my life. I made him realize his comment wasn't just a comment but the last drop of water that made the bathtub spill over. But dimpled dude was just a desk clerk; there was nothing else he could really do. He couldn't undo my hurt or upgrade me to first class or give me free flights for life, the only thing he controlled were hotel vouchers and the food coupons. He gave me extra food coupons, not, I hoped, to add insult to my injury, but I believe it was the only thing he had open to him to make amends.

I headed out to the Airport Ramada shuttle, where a nice man in a business suit told me the airline worker was out of line. For a brief second, I imagined having sex with him at the Airport Ramada, but then he took a call from his wife. "Hi, honey. Yep. Stuck in Atlanta."

As soon as we got to the motel, I ate pepperoni pizza from a vending machine which I heated up in a dirty microwave and Famous Amos cookies for dinner. And I didn't care because I was apparently eating for two . . .

COWORKER PHONE SEX

During the first week of a new gig, which I shall not name (you'll see why soon enough), the entire writing staff went on a retreat. Retreats are basically a way to drink without having to drive home and a way to get your new writers to work a ton of hours without the distraction of their loving and needy wives/husbands/children. We went to Vegas, which was good for the drinking but not as good for the writing. We went out the first night and got smashed, the most common way of course to bond with new coworkers. I was the only woman in a group of mostly married men. But I was just one of the guys . . . or so I thought. At about three o'clock in the morning, after we'd closed out the bars, the phone rang in my hotel room.

I answered groggily. "Hello?"

A vaguely familiar voice said, "It's me."

It was Phil—a tall, lanky married coworker with a couple of kids. I asked him what he wanted.

He paused and then began, "So, you know when you asked if any of us had done ecstasy? Well, I lied. I have done it." Earlier in the night at a bar, the topic of drugs had come up. I asked if anyone had done ecstasy, and what it was like for them. The idea of it is amazing. Love everything. Love yourself. Nobody admitted doing it. Maybe it was too early in our collective relationship. We didn't know if we could trust each other. But clearly it was not too early for Phil. Or at least not to early to tell me . . . on the phone . . . at three o'clock in the morning when all I wanted to do was go to sleep or watch still-in-the-theatre movies.

Phil lowered his voice and started to tell me a lewd tale about the sexiest girls you could imagine, with legs for days, approaching him at a college keg party with this new drug ecstasy.

After a beat he took the temperature, "I haven't even told my wife this." Married guys love to tell you stuff they haven't told their wives.

I didn't take the bait. "Really? Huh."

I was awake at that point, but had no idea where this was going. When we'd gotten back to the hotel from the bar, Phil and I were at the elevator bank. He was going down and I was going up, he asked me if I was sure he should go down. I had no idea what he meant. He was not my type and I would never do anything with a guy who was married. Not only married, but somebody's daddy.

The daddy continued with his story, his voice dropping lower and lower as he went. "So, the girls and I took two ecstasy pills each and went to the movies. There was nobody there. And they proceeded to kiss me. And then one went down on me and I went down on the other. Then they were kissing each other, soft on the mouth. Looking back at me to make sure I was watching. I was watching and touching myself and it was so exciting and nobody was around but somebody could have walked in at any moment."

I didn't know what to say. I felt like I had fallen asleep and dreamed Penthouse Forum. In the most professional tone I could muster at three o'clock in the morning to a new coworker trying to have semi-phone sex with me.

I said, "Wow. That's a funny story."

———————

It wasn't funny. It was inappropriate. It was not what I wanted to be doing the night before we were about to meet our new boss/lead actor for the first time, where I would have to be both cute and convincing that I could write comedy even though I was a woman.

Phil didn't seem to take the signal of my professionalism. He kept going, "Then we go back to their place and I have sex with both of them, every hole. At any given point I am in something or something is in me."

I didn't ask any follow-up questions. I just let him go on until I told him it was late and that we had to get up early. He agreed.

The next morning I expected him to be embarrassed, but he wasn't. I was. Sometimes I am sad to be a woman. Sad to have to deal with guys like Phil. And sad that guys like Phil have no idea they are guys like Phil.

When we got back to L.A., things didn't change. He called me when his wife was out of town and stopped by my office when no one was around. He was aggressively passive in what he wanted from me. I don't think he wanted to do anything, but he certainly wanted to talk about doing it.

There was a blackout at the studio one day. He crept into my office and leaned into me, with his leg pressed hard against mine and whispered in my ear what he fantasized about doing. I just sat there and listened like he was telling me what he was going to order for lunch. Or what he thought the weekend's weather would be. He thought I was turned on. But I was really just interested in the attention. He didn't make me feel like I wanted to have sex with him but he did make me feel sexy.

I don't know why I answered the phone when Phil called. Why I sat through things like this:

Phil would say, "So, how wet are you?"

I would pause and then say something casual like, "I don't know how wet are you?" In the same tone I would say, "I don't know, what do you want for dinner?"

My voice would be firm and cold and still something made it impossible for me to hang up. It's like walking by construction workers. You don't want them to hoot, but if they don't you're hurt because there is clearly something you like about it.

One night, a few writers went to a really dark bar that had strong drinks with pineapple skewers and terrible Chinese food with certain heartburn. Phil and I were the last ones left at the end of the evening; everyone else had spouses they actually wanted to get home to. Phil was ordering drinks made to mask the taste of alcohol from girls; they made his lips loose and want to discuss his favorite subject, my ass.

I told him it was too big.

He was shocked, "C'mon, you know what a great ass you have. You know what you're doing when you come in to work with those tight jeans on." His tone was accusing. I told him I had no idea what I was doing. If I did then I wouldn't spend so much money on Snack Well's and Slim-Fast shakes and so much time hating myself.

It was late at that point. And as always, he wrapped up our interaction with a warning. He'd warn me that I could never tell anyone about "us." His precious wife he swore he loved would leave him. He would never work in this town again. I stopped listening, stuck wondering what he thought *we* were.

Phil parked far away from the restaurant in a Trader Joe's parking lot down a street known for transvestite hookers. I drove him there in my black VW Jetta that smelled like crayons. Before he got out he leaned over and grabbed one of my boobs.

I finally found my legs and said, "Phil, I think this has gone too far."

He knew I was right. His hand was still on my breast. Before removing his hand he gave it a quick squeeze. He got out of the car. A few weeks later the job was over. And so were "we."

WHAT DO YOU THINK
OF MY BOOBIES?

Being in a long-term relationship has its advantages. You get a warm person to snuggle in bed with, who you can tell anything to because there aren't any boundaries. You can freely toot in your sleep without worrying the guy will never call you again. When you're in a relationship, you also have a partner to do things with you that you can't do alone or it would seem pathetic and sad (eat McDonald's for three meals in one day, watch an entire *Real World* marathon in bed or dust your Beanie Babies). All things I've done alone and know from experience are pathetic and sad. But the biggest advantage to having a boyfriend or girlfriend is a guaranteed date on February 14th.

The first Valentine's Day after a break-up is torture. Lost, confused, and desperate are just a few of the feelings that float to the surface. You secretly hope your ex calls and at the same time pray he doesn't. You wonder if you'll ever have another Valentine's date again. You come close to sending yourself flowers but you still feel superior to your single friends. You cling to the knowledge that someone did in fact love you as proof it can happen again. And the faster it happens again the better. In low moments when I feel like the only people who love me are my parents, I think about something my dermatologist once told me, "Fungus loves you." That's right. No matter what happens, fungus loves me. But fungus can't make dinner on Valentine's Day.

The Valentine's Day after my relationship with Kyle ended came a week after a blind date. The blind date was my first *first* date in five years. I'd been with Kyle so long I thought I'd never have to go on a first date again. I was wrong. I needed to get out there. But even that phrase makes me want to die. "Get out there again?" What the hell is "out there"? And why can't it come in here? I'd spent six months of mourning/feeling sorry for myself/Tylenol PM/mimosas and having deep conversations with my cats.

A mutual friend set Victor and me up. They'd gone to law school together. Trustworthy friend. Good law school. Corporate lawyer. And new in town, so he was still used to dating normal women not L.A. women. There's a big difference. Normal women eat a sleeve of cookies and say, "I was so bad. Gotta be good for the rest of the day." L.A. women eat a dinner roll and want to kill themselves.

I just wanted to have a relaxed, chill attitude. I'd never felt the need to *chill* before, but I was trying new things. And no matter what happened, it was just a date. They happen everyday, all over the world, to all kinds of people. It was no big deal. But I couldn't stop my mind from drifting to things I would typically never admit to. "What if I ended up marrying Victor? That would be perfect. Then I wouldn't ever have to go on a first date again!" Part of me wanted to meet someone I could marry right away and just get it over with. If that's not romantic, I don't know what is.

We had drinks at a dark sushi bar that you probably wouldn't want to see in the light of day. We hit it off . . . enough. He wore a corduroy jacket and talked about American Indians and his dead mother. I talked about everything and nothing in particular. A second date was implied but not certain. He could *still* be my future husband.

The first post-break-up date was over and I could start to focus on post-break-up momentous occasion number two, Valentine's Day.

One of the previous Valentine's Days consisted of red roses, dinner, and a heartfelt Hallmark Mahogany greeting card to my ass. It was a lot to live up to. Victor asked me out the night before Valentine's Day and when I say *before* I mean literally about five minutes before midnight. It seemed odd, but I wasn't going to be picky under the circumstances. I wanted a Valentine. He didn't however mention Valentine's Day at all in the e-mail. Just a simple, "Dinner tomorrow night?"

We decided to meet at his place because it was more convenient for him. I'd rushed home from work to shower and change and in my mad panic I began sweating. It was a nervous sweat. I kept thinking it would stop but as I drove farther and farther up into the Hollywood Hills, it kept going. The sweat level was that of an overweight jogger having a heart attack while eating hot sauce in the desert. I alternated the air vents of the VW Jetta at my armpits and temples. I drove slow and prayed to the dating gods for help. The part of my brain that wasn't on the sweat problem was hoping Victor's apartment was nice, but not nicer than mine.

I arrived at Victor's with slightly damp armpits and two wet rings covered by a sweater it was too hot to wear. Luckily you could still make out the cleavage enhancing silk paisley top I was wearing. Happy Valentine's Day. There were moving boxes everywhere. And still no actual mention of Valentine's Day. His place was nicer than mine and I obsessed about this out loud and in my head. He was cute, short, but cuter than I remembered.

Victor smiled and said, "I found out about this place with a Thai Elvis. I thought it would be fun."

I hate Thai food.

"I love Thai food!" I said with great enthusiasm, "that sounds great!"

Lies. A terrific way to start a relationship with the man I might marry.

He'd just bought a red convertible, a little douche-baggy but it was used, so I was willing to overlook it. The Thai place was crowded and loud. Surprisingly, there was also Japanese and Chinese food on the menu. I think when Asian restaurants do this it's condescending. It assumes our taste buds are racist and can't tell Pad Thai from sushi.

The Thai Elvis was not there. We ate and yelled over a few glasses of Sapporo (Japanese) and then went back to his better-than-my-place. It was a work night and I had to get up the next day and write dramedy for Nickelodeon, but I was drunk. I would be hung-over writing tween inspiration the next day and I didn't care. He got me some tap water and we made small talk on his modern couch.

Victor slid closer to me and said, "I'm taking tennis lessons with some girls from work."

I thought about how cute the girls from work were and how he was probably interested in one of them.

I said awkwardly, "So, are they sexy coworkers?"

Victor pulled away, "Are you jealous?"

I laughed, totally embarrassed. You forget that when you're dating someone for five years you can say anything, but when you're dating someone for five minutes, you can't. I think that's what I miss most about being in a long-term relationship. There really are no boundaries. You know you can say almost anything after a certain point. One time, over breadsticks at the Olive Garden, my ex told me a hurtful truth.

He said, with food in his mouth, "I think you'd make a terrible mother."

That was after a year. You can't say that kind of thing on a first date or accuse someone of liking his sexy tennis partners. Victor and I sat in silence, as I admired things not worthy of admiration.

"Nice kitchen block."

Then he took me by surprise. He grabbed me and kissed me . . . hard. A hard kiss that required him to brace himself against the straight lines of his replica mid-century couch. It's not what I was expecting but in my head I knew I had to get the first post-break-up kiss out of the way. I matched his technique as well as I could. It reminded me of kisses you saw foreign exchange students having in the back of the bus on high school field trips. We kissed long enough for me to get mashed up against the side table filled with pretentious coffee table books that were bought for their size and title not their content.

I broke loose to say, "I think I'm too drunk to drive home right now."

Victor, after a beat, said, "You can . . . stay?" His seemingly declarative sentence trailed off in a question. I ignored this.

I did stay. I put on a white undershirt of his and we made out. He was probably thinking sex. I was thinking cuddling, slumber party; one night I don't have to be alone on my deflated air mattress since my cousin still hadn't gotten me that free bed he promised. One night free from listening to my cat pee in my hallway and hoping magically that it would be gone by morning. Victor took my/his shirt off. I hadn't done any fooling around in so long I didn't know what to do. I didn't even know if I wanted to be there. I sort of wanted to lose weight and take up piano before I got into another relationship. He touched me and I missed my ex: not him, but the comfort. My thoughts raced and the room had become silent. Only the sound of two people kissing, who barely liked each other, filled the room. I felt a responsibility to break the silence.

I cleared my throat, "So . . ."

I searched desperately for something to say. I do write comedy. I could have come up with something clever, maybe even funny or sexy. I can do sexy sometimes.

What came out was, ". . . what do you think of my boobies?"

I don't think I'd used the word boobies in twenty years, but that's what came out. Full volume. Boobies! No bedroom voice. Boobies! Nothing sexy about it. Boobies! The Hollywood Hills have houses close together, so it's possible the neighbors even heard. I'd swiftly killed whatever sexual energy there was between us. Politely, he said he thought my boobies were good after a very long pause. I was beyond embarrassed. We went back to awkwardly making out, and then eventually I faked falling asleep after I made it clear we weren't doing anything else. He fell asleep. I was too worried I would toot, so I stayed awake. Sometimes when I'm staying over at a gentleman's house I'll go into the bathroom and quietly fart into a towel to avoid this problem, but I didn't want to wake him. At one point, Victor rolled over to tell me he was not a morning person and not to expect anything from him.

The sun came up and he stayed true to his word. He was cold and didn't look at me, which was good since I had make-up everywhere but where it belonged. My sexy lace tank top and high heels mocked me in the light of workday morning. Victor was busy getting ready. We kissed, lips barely touched, and I was on my way out the door. I turned around to see if he was watching me walk away and he wasn't. He'd already disappeared around the corner to prepare his breakfast on his nice kitchen block. I stood for a moment and took in the feeling. It was the feeling that maybe a Valentine's Day at home would have been better. I walked carefully down the steep, quintessential Hollywood Hills street to my car, passing a man walking his small dog, wondering where my ex was waking up and if he missed my "good" boobies.

THE PRE-FAMOUS DUDE

When Emmett started urinating on the carpet in the hallway, I'd put shower curtains down at night and he would pee on those. Thank God for IKEA or I'd have no savings. Without a boyfriend or roommate or friend who was over regularly to see this shower curtain horror show, this indoor urine Slip N' Slide, I was able to convince myself that it was an acceptable human living situation. It was not, however, and I knew I needed to get out into the world and socialize before I became a weird cat lady shut-in.

My friend Kelly invited me to a St. Patrick's Day party that was within walking distance from my house. She called it "hook-up central." It went all day and into the night. More booze than you could imagine. I figured if I was going to venture out into the world, free booze and easy hook-ups was a good place to start.

When I got to the party my friend asked me what type of guy I was looking for. I said "nerd." A few minutes later, I was getting a drink and a guy walked in with short black hair, thrift-store clothes, and a slightly scrawny but tall tan body, and without even introducing herself to him Kelly yelled at me across the yard.

"Hilary, I got your guy!"

We talked. He was really funny and I'm not going to lie, so was I. He brought out the funny in me. It turned out we had friends in common (Hollywood is a small town) so we both knew the other person was okay. Legit. Certified. It's very similar to dogs sniffing each other's asses at the park. But he was cuter than a dog's ass. After a few hours he asked me what my "situation" was. He'd recently gotten out of a long-term relationship. So had I! He wasn't looking for a commitment and for once in my life, neither was I! I needed to just date for a while. We made a deal. One fun night and that was it. He asked me to go to another party with him. In my head I had already skipped passed the party and was worried about whose place we'd end up at. I wondered if the shower curtains were down for Emmett to pee on.

We went to the other side of town to a dive bar not worth the drive. We made out openly in front of people who probably didn't want to see that. I tried to match my technique to his. I was drunk and so was he but not quite drunk enough not to be embarrassed by openly making out in public. I got that. We went outside to the residential neighborhood that surrounded this tiny pub. We sat on the hard cold curb going at it like pre-teens. We reminded each other, "One shot, one night."

We rode back to my place, his sober and probably irritated roommate in skinny jeans at the wheel. We were in the backseat and he held my hand, which he also announced to his roommate. Nobody had held my hand since Kyle, and he probably didn't do it the last year we dated.

When we got back to my apartment I went in first to make sure everything seemed normal and inhabitable. He was the first guy who'd been to my post-Kyle pad. We went to the bedroom to finish what we'd started. It was sloppy but fun. We laughed and smiled at each other and ourselves. He kept asking if I had condoms even though we'd made a pact not to have sex. I reminded him, and a few minutes later he asked again. We fell asleep, but as usual I was afraid I'd toot, so I kept waking up. He slept soundly. At some point Emmett jumped up on the bed and nudged in between us. He woke up and saw the cat.

I said, as crazy as you imagine it sounding, "Isn't Emmett handsome?"

He took a deep breath, "Don't make me say that."

I nodded. That was fair. He *is* handsome though. The guy dozed off again and I ran into the hall and cleaned up the cat pee on the shower curtain, went into the bathroom and tried to apply makeup that looked like it was still on from the night before in a good way. After an hour or so of obligatory talking about nothing important and me trying to stay in a position where my boobs still look good, he got up to leave. The Pre-Famous Dude didn't know what to say to end the "affair."

He said, "Should we exchange info?"

I shook my head. I didn't want to "exchange info." We had a plan. We weren't going to stay in touch so nobody got hurt or rejected. We pre-rejected each other. He wrote his number down anyway and took mine. I knew I wouldn't be using it. I stuck by my decision. I think he just felt weird leaving without some way to contact each other.

He said good-bye and I smiled. I felt like I'd had a true adult experience. I wasn't grabbing on to him and not letting go like a kid with their mom on the first day of kindergarten. I wasn't obsessing over what he thought of me. It was what it was.

A few days later the dude called me, "I can't date you."

I said, "I know, it's too soon for me too. Remember? We agreed, one night. We made a deal."

I didn't expect or want to date him. We had a plan. And I wanted "cool girl" credit for that. But he continued on about how it was bad timing and he wasn't ready and he "broke up" with me even though I didn't want anything more from him. The language he used was meant to be gentle and reassuring to the person he was letting down easy but I didn't need to be let down. I hadn't expected to hear from him ever again. He ignored my responses and mowed me down with his one-sided break-up. Then it seemed like he wanted credit for being a good honest guy.

"Yeah, so that's it. Just wanted to be honest with you."

"Um, yeah. Thanks for calling."

"I'm sorry about this."

"Don't be. One day we'll run into each other at a party and we'll think about how we saw each other naked once and that will be our little secret."

"Cool. Again, sorry to be lame."

"Not lame."

"Bye."

And with that frustrating phone call I learned the lesson that there is no such thing as a pre-rejection, but there is such thing as a post-rejection.

A few months after our encounter, the nerdy dude became wickedly famous. Everyone in America knew his name overnight from a huge box office hit. Friends kept e-mailing me about him. His movie. His upcoming TV show. Have I heard of this guy? He's so brilliant. He's so handsome. He's the next big thing.

So now when I see him in a gossip rag at the Supermarket linked to a Hollywood starlet or on the big screen at a movie theatre, I turn and look at the people around me and smugly think to myself, "I've seen that dude naked."

LOLLY'S ACNE

I have never felt more single than the night I stayed in to apply Pro-Activ and a warm compress to my cat's acne ridden chin.

THE ACCIDENTAL HAND JOB

There's always that one real catch in your circle of friends who's never single when you're single. But you just know there's something there. And even though you're desperate to hook up with each other, your love lives are completely opposite. He's falling into love as you're burying it. And he breaks up with her just as you're into someone new yourself. When you run into him at parties you attend with your boyfriend, your thoughts drift to what it would be like if he were the one taking you home. You see him thinking that too when he's with his new love and you just went on a break-up diet and look awesome. His girlfriends always distrust you for good reason. And your boyfriends never invite him out for a beer. Now, if you felt like you were soul mates you'd take drastic action but you know in your heart of hearts you really just want one night together. It's an unfair cycle, cupid conspiring against lust. But every once in a while cupid is not paying attention, hung-over, or napping, when the unthinkable happens. At two separate apartments, in two separate relationships, in two separate cities, someone says, "It's over." And all of a sudden anything is possible. That's what happened with Ray.

Ray and I met in a Groundlings improv class. I was in a relationship and he was off limits but that didn't keep me from laughing extra hard at his scenes. He's a preppy caveman! He's a German air controller made of cotton candy! He's the President delivering a baby on the moon! Hilarious! Ray had this permanent smirk and these incredible deep dark Middle Eastern eyes that seemed to contain secrets he'd never told anyone but might tell me. He was short but he'd once been a bouncer at a bar. He didn't need the height to get his message across, not Ray. I could just see it, him charming rowdy patrons with his wit and wry smile. He told another guy in the class he thought I was cute. From that point on, I was in and the countdown began.

Even when I was packing up boxes and moving out of the house Kyle and I lived in, I thought about Ray. I was single again but I heard he was dating someone and living in New York. The cycle continued three thousand miles away. A few guys came and went. None of them were anything more than a way to pass the time. None of them had eyes with secrets. At least not secrets I cared about knowing. And then it happened. Ray was back in town. He'd been writing for a late night show, he described as "Comedy Vietnam." But it was over now. Not entirely mutual, but for the best. Just like my relationship. And guess whom he'd lost in the move? His girlfriend. It was a miracle. I made plans to meet him for *a* drink. I hoped it would be more like eighteen drinks.

There was excitement in the air. I entered the extremely dark, extremely trendy bar and there he was. He looked like the perfect him. I looked like the perfect me. It was a recipe for a perfect night. Nothing could go wrong. I ordered a gin and tonic, the adult Sprite. Since I hadn't eaten in anticipation of putting on my favorite jeans, I knew it would hit me hard. Good. I hoped Ray hadn't eaten either.

There was a connection and a level of comfort between the two of us. I didn't have to impress him, because the groundwork had already been laid. Ray told me he was *newly* single, like I didn't know. We talked casually about my ex. Ray never really liked him, and thought I deserved better. For all intents and purposes that was his pick-up line. I got drunk. He got drunk. We both knew where it was going. I guess it's what a guy feels like when he hires an escort. He meets her out, they have some drinks, she laughs at jokes that aren't even funny, but they both know what's going to happen in the end. We left the bar, and my car parked on the street, to head back to his house up the winding roads of Echo Park.

Ray lived with a bunch of guys. His house had a kind of group home feel. Rag-tag furniture, Post-it notes on the phone, people coming in and out in various stages of inebriation. Luckily, he had his own room with a view of the freeway, which in L.A. is still a view. There was one chair but we sat on the bed. The "bed" was just a mattress on the floor. He was too old to have a mattress on the floor and live in a situation where you have to label your food in the fridge. But I didn't want to marry him.

The energy was electric. Our bodies weren't even touching and I felt like I was buzzing. Then mid-unimportant sentence he rolled over, grabbed my shoulders, and we were kissing. Take that cupid. Finally. We'd waited for years and now we'd done it. It felt like it wasn't supposed to happen and that maybe by us being together were going to open some sort of portal into another universe. I was lost in the kiss for a few minutes, my head swirling like it does before I pass out from not eating breakfast. Then I started to come to.

Ray was kissing me hard and fast. And I realized it wasn't good at all. In fact, it was terrible. Was I bad or was he? I was not giving up. This was our one night. Before we both knew it we'd be in other relationships and the window would be closed. We had to make this count.

I got on top of him. Then he got on top of me. Things started to improve. We got more in sync. My neck got un-squished and his tired arm found a pillow to rest on. The kissing got less hard and panicked. We weren't worried anymore that the other person was going to disappear like a dream. The kissing relaxed. This was my chance to show Ray I was everything he imagined in our little improv class. And leave him with something to think about the next time we ran into each other at a party with someone else on our arm.

There was a little over-the-shirt action, which turned to under-the-shirt. I skipped over-the-pants and went straight to under-the-pants. My plan: a little appetizer hand job. A little ninth grade shout-out. A little "naughty but still nice" kind of a thing. I thought, "This is going to be great. What a way to start the night." Then as quickly as it started, "WHAM!" It was over. Over over.

I was confused and sat for a second with my hands still down his pants. He seemed to be done off of just that. Off that innocent move. He probably would have gotten more friction on the Indiana Jones ride at Disneyland. He rubbed my arms as if to thank me and say, "You can take your hands out of my pants now." After a moment of silence for the night that was apparently not going to be, I pulled my hand reluctantly out of his still-buttoned jeans. I was in shock, *Could it really be over?* Then I decided there would be a round two. Yes, a round two. He must just be taking a breather before he works himself up again. Then Ray fell asleep and I fell into hysteria.

I knew before that we weren't going to date, be boyfriend and girlfriend. But I was worried this was it, the last time I'd have a chance to show the handsome, charming Ray what it's like to be with *me*. I mean for God's sake we have friends in common. What if I wanted to date one of his buddies in the future and when asked for a review Ray says, "Eh. A little too into the hand jobs." I didn't even get a chance to use the tips I've picked up from ex-boyfriends ("more ball-play") and casual hook-ups ("no slumber parties without sex"). Then he rolled over. *Okay,* I thought, *Here we go.* Ray leaned in and gave me peck on the forehead. He thought the appetizer was the entrée.

It was official. I'd accidentally given the most eligible bachelor in my life a measly hand job. Ray was going to leave that night thinking that was my big move. That I was a twenty-eight-year-old hand job queen. He must not have been shocked my ex broke up with me. Who gives H.J.'s as the main course? It was humiliating. I didn't realize I needed to provide a menu of what was going to be served.

Ray slept like baby and I couldn't sleep. Remember nobody had gone down my pants. But that didn't matter to me. An H.J. was exchanged. That's what the record would show. My mascara and eyeliner were smeared all over my face and I was out of breath-freshening gum or mints that I would surely need in the morning. And to make matters worse I had to pee. Ray's bathroom was filthy and I had to lay down Kleenex from my purse onto the toilet seat. While I was in the bathroom, I heard some of his roommates come home. They headed to the kitchen to most certainly devour snacks with someone else's name on them. Hopefully Ray's.

I hurried back to Ray's bedroom and the sun was starting to come up over the freeway. The sky was pink and cars passed each other going in opposite directions. Some were ending the night, some were starting the day. But most definitely my night was over. Our night was over. A little while later, Ray woke up. We got dressed. I tucked my extra ten/fifteen/twenty pounds into my jeans. Without many words, he drove me back to the bar on Sunset where I'd left my car and my sobriety the night before. We hugged politely. He waited for me to get in my Jetta and that was it. I drove away with only an accidental hand job under my belt and a fantasy ruined. I guess the universe had the last laugh after all.

HOW A LEAN CUISINE SPA MEAL RUINED THE PERFECT HOOK-UP

One of my closest friends, Maya, broke up with her ex-college-football-player husband the same week Kyle and I broke up. Kyle and the husband were buddies from college. We were their dysfunctional couple best friends. We indulged each other in bad behavior. "See what he does?!" "Who only eats at Islands Burgers and Chili's?!" "She barely ever wants to fuck." "Is murder really wrong?" Our evenings often involved yelling, crying, hurt feelings, political arguments, moral questions, board games, and fried things.

Luckily, the two of us had each other to get through the breakups. Two new single ladies on the scene. Maya was going through her acting out stage around the same time I was, which was convenient. Maya invited me to a pot-"lucky" dinner party at a coworker's house. The purpose was for Maya's friend to set her up with a few guys so she could get lucky, have some fun. I was told that she got first pick and that I could take her leftovers. A fair and sad commentary of single life in your late twenties/early thirties. But I agreed. An even sadder commentary on single life in your late twenties/early thirties. But it's hard to resist the perfect hook-up. A vouched-for person who is attractive and just looking to have a good night. A string-free hook-up that doesn't have to involve sex but certainly doesn't involve feelings or phone calls the next day.

We arrived at the cute two-story townhouse in Venice, right along the canals, a half-hour late. It felt beach-y and hip and far away from my Hollywood cave covered in cat urine and sadness. We were both nicely dressed with bottles of wine and Japanese ice cream. Of course I was trying to lose weight as usual, so by the time we get there all I'd had to eat was an Organic Lean Cuisine Spa Meal and lettuce.

It was about the third glass of wine prior to eating anything that I realized I was in trouble. I was in trouble because 1) I was already drunk an hour in and 2) everyone else was too. The host was married and everyone else was single. Maya chose a guy early on, but of course I was only attracted to the married one. He was flirty but so in love with his wife. I was attracted to that affection he had for his wife more than him. The night got loud and fondue was served late and there wasn't enough of it. And the little I got was no match for the entire bottle of Cab Sav in my stomach.

We were all laughing and drinking and dancing and laughing and drinking and flirting and did I mention drinking? I think there was a game of charades. I think there were deep conversations. I know there was Absinthe. And I know a tall skinny guy arrived late. I don't think I ever got his name but he was a TV editor, he was single, and my friend had already picked her horse. In fact, she already had her tongue in her horse's mouth. After drunken small talk about your guess is as good as mine, we went out on the small rusty balcony (potential disaster) that had two chairs and too many plants in various stages of death. He started kissing me. See, the perfect hook-up.

Then, as uncooly as I could possibly say it, I managed to get out, "I'm going to be sick now!"

I ran through the apartment to the bathroom, and threw up many things, things I didn't remember eating. Fondue. Wine.

Cookies. Something that looked like a yogurt lid. I came out and found the entire dinner party standing outside the bathroom door. It felt like a murder mystery party, and I was the one with the clue. I did it in the bathroom, on my knees, holding my own hair.

In the voice of an official declaration I announced upon exit, "It's okay. Everyone, it's okay. I just threw up a Lean Cuisine Spa Meal. They're organic." That last bit of information seemed important for some reason.

I stumbled back to the couch and disappeared into its cushions that had lost all their firmness and were just sacks of down. My friend disappeared to the back bedroom. The hosts disappeared to their bedroom. The single men who lost took their ball and went home. On the couch, the editor put a throw blanket over me and started to kiss me again.

"Dude," I say, both repulsed and disappointed, "I just threw up."

He held me anyway. Damn you Lean Cuisine Spa Meal for ruining the perfect hook-up.

THE "I-CAN'T-BELIEVE-I-LIVE-ON-THE-BEACH" GUY

I don't know if you're familiar with the MTV reality dating show genre, but I had a brief stint of employment working on one. It involved young men going on dates with moms, who then picked one of the guys to date her daughter. It was pre–the word "cougar" but I saw that trend coming. A lot of heavily lip-glossed women crammed into cropped white pants with upper arms jiggling as they laughed at the young guys' dumb jokes. It was barely a writing job, but it got me out of the house while I worked on getting a more legitimate gig. The show was pretty much run by kids. They paid so little that people without mortgages and a need for health insurance were the only ones who could afford to work there. It was just what I was looking for, a bunch of young people looking for something to fill their nights off. We worked long days and yet people always seemed up to go out afterwards. It was perfect, because I was looking for a guy to sleep with. The first guy after Kyle. The guy who would help me prove to myself that I was healed. I found Jackson.

Jackson worked in casting helping to choose the moms. The way they treated him you'd think he'd cast them in *The English Patient 2*. They adored him and the experience. You could see them soaking up every last detail to share at their next Orange County pool party.

None of us were making art, but we still tried to do the best we could. Jackson had a cute smile and was single and that was all that really mattered to me at that point. It was clear after a few days on set that something was going to happen. The Kyle wound was still raw, but I knew Jackson could help. I manipulated him. I laughed out loud at jokes that I didn't really get but I knew from the tone *he* thought they were jokes. I wore tube tops, bought specifically for him. They were tight on the boobs and then went out over the pooch. He was everything Kyle wasn't. And he told me he lived on the beach. Kyle would never live on the beach.

All Jackson and I did for a few dates was make out, sloppily, in front of too many people. It was hard for me to be around him and not be drinking; we didn't really have a special connection. We were just two single people looking to touch each other's sexy parts. I know that sounds crass, but isn't that just the plain truth? And is there anything wrong with that? I guess I didn't know; I'd never really done that before.

Jackson clearly wanted more than just a little kissie-face and it was clear he was going to have to instigate the next level (sex). There was nothing else for us to do together. I didn't want to talk about anything important. I didn't want him to really know me. He was a recreational drug: better the first couple of times you do it. One night, after drinking of course, we stumbled back home and into his room. We rolled around on his neatly made bed and then made our way under the covers.

I said, "You know I'm not sure that I'm really ready to have sex with you. With anyone. I mean it hasn't been that long since Kyle. And I'm just unsure and confused. Sex might not be best the thing for me right now."

Jackson looks at me confused. "We're already having sex."

I was clearly a little drunk. Turns out we were in the middle of the act. My body was saying one thing and my heart was saying something else. I wished my heart could be more of a slut. Then maybe the break-up wouldn't have hurt so badly.

Without fail every morning Jackson would wake up, pour a cup of coffee in his kitchen, and crane to see a tiny sliver of beach from the kitchen window. He would smile and say, "I can't believe I live on the beach." Jackson loved the beach. And to him this was living. His apartment was decorated in a palm tree/monkey theme. He kept it impeccably clean. There was a beer fridge next to the couch.

I only let Jackson come to my apartment in Hollywood once (he left his watch) and he never met any of my friends. I hid him like a bottle of liquor in the laundry hamper under a pile of dirty clothes. One night I met him and his guy friends for drinks and ate fried things from the ocean in a basket and drank seasonal beers. They watched suspiciously as he kissed me and put his arms around me. They were right to be suspicious; I was not really there for him. I was there for me. I needed to sleep with a guy after Kyle who I didn't care about. Jackson was nice. He was simple. He was sweet. He was Southern. He was more into me.

One Saturday night, we sat across from each other at a midrange Mexican restaurant, slamming frozen Margaritas despite the painful brain freeze consequences, hoping there was a conversation starter at the bottom.

The margaritas did create a conversation. The conversation was about sex, bumping uglies, knocking boots, and the fact that we were going to "do it." We headed back to his immaculate pad that surprisingly always had toilet paper, not on the floor but actually in the holder. I've been in way too many single guys' bathrooms and I can tell you this is a rarity. I was a little unsteady on our walk home. I blamed the stacked wedge heels and not the eighty margaritas. Jackson looked down the long sloping streets towards the beach.

"I can't believe I live on the beach."

I couldn't believe I was with this guy. I looked at passing couples, seemingly so happy, as if I was a kidnapped child, hoping to be noticed by someone who saw my picture on a milk carton. Nobody rescued me. I'd created this situation.

We went back to his apartment and had the sex. It was mediocre as always. I'm not blaming him; very possibly it was my fault. I was just happy to have sex with someone other than Kyle. It was also nice to be in a clean bed with someone rubbing my back. Jackson made his bed every morning. It was a small thing, but it was the best thing about him. We fell asleep in the clean sheets.

The next morning Jackson came in with a cup of coffee. He sighed happily. "I can't believe I live on the beach."

Something snapped in my head. I wanted to scream in his face. "I can believe you live on the fucking beach because you say it every fucking day." I didn't say this. But I felt mad that he was so clueless. I was mad at myself for being there. I was embarrassed that his friends knew I wasn't really into him. Suddenly, it was over. I couldn't do it anymore. I wondered how I ended up in the bed of a man I didn't love or even like that much, covered in pillows with monkeys and palm trees. In a room where there were no books, not one. I gathered up my stuff. Left my toothbrush so he wouldn't suspect anything and gave the watch he left at my house to Goodwill. I guess I'd always known what it felt like to be used but this was the first time I felt what it was like to use.

THE TEXAS TITTY TWISTER

I briefly reunited with a college crush in my late twenties, Marco, who said he'd known since the day he'd met me freshman year that I was "the one." It was intoxicating to think the guy I was supposed to be with was someone I'd already met! Freshman year! But when we had sex, Marco couldn't finish unless I twisted his nipples . . . hard. In elementary school there was a kid named Mitchell Gomez who used to go around twisting girls' nipples and saying, "Texas Titty Twister." This is what I thought of the few times I had to do that twisting. Marco was tall, tan, Latin, and smart, but way too much work.

WHORE BATH

When I started sleeping with Dennis, I didn't tell anyone. He wasn't married or a convicted felon but it wouldn't have gone over well with my friends. He was a professional gambler and had a ridiculous lifestyle filled with drugs, drinks, bookies, late nights, and people your parents would say are bad influences and would be right. But he hid all that under conservative striped Polo shirts and sensible loafers. He was ridiculously handsome, tall, and strawberry blonde, and he made everything in me tingle. But it was a bad tingle, the kind of tingle you get when you know you're doing something wrong. Something that will later end up a story in your book.

He first tricked me into his bed by saying he'd Tivoed a really great *Cops* episode in the bedroom, "Tased and Confused." I guess I should have known we wouldn't watch the whole thing. His room was littered with reminders of all the women he'd been with before, women he'd used the same trick on. He had a drawer full of condoms of every variety. He had drawers full of things he got drunk and bought on eBay (antique keys, who buys antique keys?). I found this endearing because I'm fucked up. He had a mysterious cell phone that rang at every hour.

I'd ask nonchalantly, "Oh, who's that?"

He wouldn't give me an answer, just an I-don't-think-you-want-to-go-there look. He couldn't tell a story that didn't involve somebody he'd slept with. Often he'd say "friend" and he meant, "girl I banged." He even has a lost and found—earrings, underwear, shirts, etc. Stupid girls always leave stuff at guys' apartments so they have a reason to call. I was embarrassed for them.

After dating Dennis for several months, I asked him to come over one night, which he'd only done once. We were always at his place, because I liked him more than he liked me. First I invited him for dinner, then when that failed, a drink, and then when that failed, sex. I invited him over for sex. After three rejections I hung up the phone, crawled in my bed, and yelled at the top of my lungs for all of the West Coast to hear, "What are you doing? You are being an asshole! He can't give you want you want!" This guy was like eating an entire box of Thin Mints in the morning on the way to work and then telling everyone you had a Slim Fast shake. He made me lie to myself. He made me nauseous and want to have sex with him all at the same time. If I could make love to him and throw up at the same time I might have satisfied the feeling he created in me. But I couldn't give him up.

One morning I woke up on his stiff white hotel-like sheets with his blackout curtains hiding daylight. I'd set the alarm early so I could stop and get breakfast before work. He rubbed my back but it felt obligatory. He said the right things but with the wrong emotion. I felt the ghosts of all the girls who had been there before warning me. Dennis was anxious for me to leave. Him rubbing my back might as well be him pushing me toward the door, out the door, and on the street in his newly gentrified East side neighborhood, so he could return those late night phone calls and text messages. I told him I needed to shower before work.

Dennis said casually, "Do you just want to take a whore bath?"

A whore bath is where you just clean the special really dirty spots. Usually between customers, I'm guessing.

Taken aback, I countered, "Can't I just take a regular bath?"

———————

He nodded after a beat, but it was clear they were all whore baths to him. I took my regular bath and then left, after leaving a pair of silver dangly hoop earrings behind so he would have to see me again. Because I was looking for a guy who would treat me the way I felt inside.

BIRTHDAY BATH WITH A STRANGER

For my twenty-ninth birthday, I decided to have a party at an incredibly happening hotel bar in downtown L.A., but because I was not incredibly happening I had to start the party at five so I could get in. The bar was on the roof and you could see all of downtown, twinkling lights and beautiful buildings that don't tell the story that is really going down on the homeless-filled streets below. The roof was covered in Astroturf, bold colored uncomfortable modern furniture, and attractive girls who look like a million bucks but drive falling-apart Mazdas they are embarrassed to park at valet. The night was a blur of champagne and raspberry vodka, and making out with two guys. One of whom I recently ran into at a business meeting. Another of whom I don't remember and was witnessed by a partygoer. This is the kind of party you have at twenty-three, not twenty-nine. At twenty-nine people have children, people I know.

We closed down the bar and I lost all my cohorts except for one random actor dude, who came with some people I invited, and my best friend who I'd gotten a room with at the hotel. Actor dude had a name I could not remember and had a mop of shaggy chestnut colored hair and eyes that wanted an adventure. We headed down to the suite I'd rented.

The hotel was a cool modern artsy hotel that had a giant bath-tub in the middle of the room. I'd had so many drinks at that point

I felt like I was watching the world through a swimming pool. Since we weren't going to be having a threesome, it was kind of an awkward situation. I did the most logical thing a drunk person could do. I raided the mini-bar and began drawing a bath. Who wouldn't want to take a bath at two-thirtyish in the morning?

My very good and understanding buddy excused herself and pretended to go to sleep, while I heated the water up for random guy and me. I put my bathing suit on; it seemed like the lady-like thing to do. He got in his boxers, the gentlemanly thing to do. We sat in the bath as it rose. We made out a little bit under the running water, but mostly we just soaped up and enjoyed the bath. Once the water got cold we got out. He held me shaking in a towel in the room that was a temperature that had been set hours earlier during the heat of the day. We watched infomercials and talked quietly about things we thought we should talk about after taking a bath together. He grew up in New Jersey. A few hours later, random guy was out the door. We exchanged numbers but we knew we would never call each other. We were just two grown adults, strangers, who took a bath together. Looked like my twenties were ending just in time.

WHAT'S UP WITH ALL THE BATHS?

I don't really know, so your guess is as good as mine. And please, if you have a guess, write me an e-mail at hilaryewinston@gmail.com and tell me what you think.

PART 5

TERRIBLE, HORRIBLE, NO GOOD, VERY BAD THINGS, AND ONE CRAZY-ASS MAILMAN

MOM'S CANCER, MY DYING CAT, AND OTHER GOOD FIRST DATE TOPICS

My mom had a bad mammogram. It's what you dread. It's why you buy a pink ribbon and make purchases at stores during Breast Cancer Awareness month. You try to fend it off. Hope that you can load up your karma to fight against it but not everyone wins. More tests on the breast tissue confirmed what we already knew in our hearts. I heard the worst thing you can possibly hear out of your parent's mouth:

"It's cancer."

My friends probably started screening my calls at some point during this year because the news got worse and worse. I don't blame them. I wouldn't want to take my calls. I didn't want to be me. I wanted to fast forward my life and see the end result. I felt utterly alone and wished to God that I were religious.

In middle school I went to a Christian sports camp. We played basketball or tennis or swam for Jesus during the day, and at night we heard testimonials from our counselors about how they were seduced by the God-less. In retrospect, they weren't doing much other than being normal college kids. They drank beers. Had sex outside of marriage. Lied to their parents. But at my age, that seemed like what happened after the rapture. One night the camp director sent all of us kids out into the woods. Pitch black woods. We all had to go find a special spot and sit alone. We needed to be as far away from other campers as we could. We were invited to have a conversation with Jesus Christ himself. And we weren't allowed come back until we had accepted him into our hearts.

I sat there for what felt like hours. I opened my heart and begged him to come. I begged God or Jesus or the Holy Spirit to find me in New Braunfels, Texas, in my neon green wind shorts and T-shirt that had a BMW logo on it and the words: "Jesus: The Ultimate Christian Experience." A million mosquitoes visited me that night but no God. I finally lied to myself and went back to camp. Greeted with hugs and Bible verses, I lied. For a year or two, I read the Bible everyday. I went to the Christian bookstore. Bought stickers, stationery, and shirts with scripture. Listened to music with such titles as, "Our God is an Awesome God." Man, he sure sounded awesome. And yet we never quite connected. Maybe in a newspaper somewhere there is a Missed Connection ad: "You, thirteenish, in the woods at night, BMW tee. Me, long white beard, all-knowing, creator of the universe. Liked your smile."

All I know is there was never going to be a time I needed a God more.

My mother went in to have a stage zero tumor removed. What the doctors called "baby cancer." But what they found after the surgery when they checked the margins was a hidden "invisible" tumor that was stage four. You don't have to know anything about cancer to know that a stage four tumor is a lot worse than a stage zero one. Things went from bad to hopeless. The negative thoughts were unstoppable. She is going to die. That's all that I could think about. On the phone she made a terrible joke about not letting my dad's second wife get her jewelry. I was furious. How could she joke about something like that? Classic Mom, having the completely wrong emotional reaction.

My relationship with my mother was a little strained going into the cancer since my parents didn't really respect my choice to be a writer and it had caused a lot of fundamental problems. And now I was sure she was going to die.

She had a mastectomy. The lymph nodes were clear so they just took the breast. She would have to wear what she calls a "chicken cutlet" to make her feel normal. They got the entire tumor but the real prognosis wouldn't come until six months later when they check the entire body to see if the cancer metastasized to the lungs or the bones or the brain. Cancer had already killed off one of her sisters and my favorite uncle so we knew this wait well. Mom began chemo and I read everything I could get my hands on. My friend worked at the American Cancer Society and she hooked me up with everything I needed to know about the disease I could do nothing to stop.

During chemo, my mother lost her frizzy black-peppered-with-gray hair. She was in a lot of pain. She was the color of paste, with her two dark brown eyes even more prominent than before because she had also lost her eyelashes. She looked small, short, sick. It was hard for me to look at her. One night, when I was home visiting with my sister, my mom came out of the bedroom without a bandana around her bald head and my sister and I yelled at her.

"You can't do that without warning!"

Our anger was out of fear. The thing that was unsaid was, "Don't leave us without a mother." There wasn't a day that I didn't feel sick right along with her, I felt perpetually sick because we were all just waiting. When my mom first started chemo she kept bragging about how much weight she was losing.

"Guess who lost ten pounds on chemo?"

She was so proud of the clothes she was fitting into. "A small!" I'll admit I was jealous but more than jealous I was angry. Why wasn't she taking this seriously? *Maybe you'll be an extra-small when you die!* But I guess she was just taking the good and running with it. We *had* been short on good.

Once your mother has cancer you should never screen her phone calls, in theory.

My mom had to go through chemo for six months. It was going to be a long wait. But my Job-like life at the time refused to wait. Refused to hold off on another plague. I was vulnerable. I was depressed. I was single. I had a cat who wouldn't stop peeing on the carpet.

My mother had cancer and my apartment was now filled with tarps and shower curtains. Not a few. Filled. My cat Emmett was supposed to get the idea to pee on these instead of the carpet but he'd started finding a way around them. I'd stopped having guests over and started having nervous breakdowns.

I'd gotten my first big writing break, on the NBC series, *My Name is Earl*. I was a low-level writer and still trying to prove myself. Your first big job makes or breaks you. My mom started her chemo on my first day. Writing comedy is difficult on a good day (perpetual self-doubt mixed with self-hatred); trying to write jokes while fielding calls about chemo and medical ports and blood tests and wills was nearly impossible. At home, I didn't have any energy for Emmett. I felt like everything in my life was on one of those cliffs that are one big earthquake away from disappearing. And there had been a lot of little earthquakes.

Emmett's situation escalated to a point where he could no longer walk and we had to go to the vet. She told me Emmett was probably having renal failure and that I might need to put him down the next day. I took him home for one last night.

I stared into Emmett's innocent green eyes and thought about getting him stuffed by a taxidermist. I took pictures. Action shots, with a feather teaser. Shots on the couch Kyle had refused to pay for. Eating treats with my other cat, Lolly. Lolly is the kind of cat only a mother could love. Neurotic. Needy. Anxious. Scared. But Emmett is even loved by cable guys and dogs. Emmett tried to move around but he couldn't. His back legs barely worked. I cried and hugged him. I admired his silver gray fur, which had lost its sheen and was covered in kitty dandruff—very similar to human dandruff. I recounted great memories of the three of us. Wondered how life was going to make up for a birthday week like this?

A few days earlier we had the premiere of *My Name is Earl* on NBC. During a celebratory lunch I got a call from my dad. My dad rarely calls me and if he does it is usually with bad news or questions about my mom's Christmas present. It was September; I knew it wasn't good. He said my mom was in the hospital with heart pains from the chemo. Apparently chemo drugs can weaken the heart and cause a heart attack. I stood outside the sushi restaurant hearing this info while I got a funny text from one of my coworkers inside. They felt terrible when they found out what was happening. I didn't know what to do, because there was nothing to do. I just took a deep breath and went back inside to push around the food I didn't even like on my plate with my chopsticks and think about my mom dying.

A few hours later, I got another call. The hospital my mom had been checked into was being evacuated because of Hurricane Rita and they had to move her. I couldn't believe this was happening. It was a few days before my birthday. I'd spent the weekend dealing with the vet and now this? I wished I believed in God so I could curse him. If he showed up in the woods at that point I would have had a few choice words for him.

Emmett stared at me weakly. He knew he was sick. Maybe he knew it was his last night. I didn't know what to do, so I made cupcakes. Strawberry cupcakes from a mix with fake little darkened red chunks inside that look like strawberries but are really just clumps of food coloring. Strawberry cake was what my mom used to always make me for my birthday when I was a kid. And might not ever make again. I made them and when they were done I sat on the couch. Emmett watched me and was obsessed with my cupcake. He loves cake and the smell triggered a deep animal hunger. He tried desperately to paw at the cupcake and it was the most energy he'd had in quite a while. I gave him one. There was no reason not to. It was his last night and we all knew it, even Lolly. I cried more tears and recounted the story of how I adopted them, when they were kittens in Virginia. I imagined they liked it because kids always love to hear the story of how they were born from their mom. This was the closest thing. I told them how I drove them home and wondered if I would be a good mom. I'd picked them up so early that the three of us took a nap together when we got home; in my lavender bedroom I had painted myself. Lolly used to fetch pennies, and when I would wake up in the morning the bed would be full of them. I finally fell asleep, with both of them on my bed not knowing what the morning was going to bring. I thought maybe it was just going to be me and Lolly and the pennies from now on.

I woke up the next day and Emmett looked worse. He was now lethargic and silent on the floor of his cage. I wished I could lay in there with him. He barely lifted his head when I called his name. I called the vet for the results of the tests, unhopeful.

"So, I have good news and bad news," the vet say cheerily. Cheer was not an emotion I had felt in a long time. "The good news is that it isn't renal failure. The bad news is that it's diabetes."

I was shocked, "I didn't know cats could get diabetes."

The vet goes on, "They can. Their insulin acts the same as ours does."

I remembered the cupcake. "Oh my God."

"What?"

Sheepishly I said, "I gave my cat a cupcake last night?"

The vet was suddenly concerned. "Why?"

I vigorously defended myself. "It was my birthday and my mom had a heart attack and there was a hurricane and I thought Emmett was dying! You told me he was dying."

The vet unmoved, says, "You should bring him in right away."

While I was waiting for the vet to come in the exam room, Emmett peed, pooped, and threw up all at the same time in my arms. A cupcake? I was right to question my mothering skills. How would I ever mother myself if my mom died? The vet grabbed Emmett. I was trying to explain and she cut me off.

"Ms. Winston, I have to go if we're going to save him."

If? I left Emmett in the care of the vet and went to work. We were trying to come up with new episodes for the show and I didn't care. I didn't care what happened to Earl and his dumb brother. What happened with his karma list of people he's wronged. All I cared about was Emmett and whether or not he was going to die. In the writers' room I nodded and pretended like I was listening to the other writers. I laughed when everyone else laughed but really was just watching my cell phone waiting for it to ring. Waiting to hear Emmett's fate. There was a terrible voice in my head, but it was a voice of reason. I knew when I got a pet I didn't want to ever keep them alive just for me. I would love them too much to let them live in pain.

My phone finally rang. I excused myself in the middle of someone's well thought out joke and took it. The vet told me Emmett was stable. I could finally breathe again. He was going to have to be put on insulin. Human insulin to be specific. Expensive human insulin. He would require insulin injections twice a day for the rest of his life. Lifespan of an indoor cat = twenty years. Emmett was only six years old. As the vet talked, I felt the panic rise up inside me. She told me that it meant a shot every twelve hours without fail. My single life flashed in front of my eyes.

"How am I supposed to do that? I work. Long hours."

The vet acted like she didn't hear me, "It's his best hope."

I pushed a little I ask, "So, it's only a hope?"

"At this point."

I imagined myself on dates telling the guy I couldn't spend the night because I had a diabetic cat at home. I imagined on nights I worked late that I would be watching the clock tick by knowing Emmett only has minutes to get his insulin shot. I imagined me having to actually give him a shot every day. Where did it go I wondered? His butt, like a kid getting a MMR vaccine? His vein? Oh, God. I thought, "Please don't let it be a vein."

Overwhelmed, I muttered, "This is a lot to handle. I need to think about this. What about one shot? Any chance one shot will do?"

The vet was giving no ground, "One shot won't work. It's a twelve hour cycle."

We got off the phone. My head was pounding with my heartbeat. I sat in the writers' room and thought about Emmett and the promise I made to myself about not keeping him alive for me.

The next day I called the doctor back, first thing in the morning.

Through tears I spoke, "Doctor, I think we need to put Emmett to sleep. I don't want to keep him alive just for me."

The vet ignored me, "The new insulin seems to be working. He's going to be okay."

"With insulin shots twice a day for the rest of his life!"

I began to cry harder. I thought about Emmett and my mother. I thought about how I'd manage to see her with a diabetic cat at home to take care of. Maybe I could go see her for twelve hours and be back in time for the shot. I wondered how I would take care of him. How I will be there for my mother? My dying cat. My dying mother. This was of course too much to burden my veterinarian with, but I didn't care.

Falling apart, I showed all my cards. "My mom has cancer. And I have to fly back and see her. She's going through chemo . . . she had a giant tumor. How do I go out of town? How do I leave Emmett? How do I live a normal life ever with my mom and Emmett sick? I'm single for God's sake. I'm alone."

The vet was silent. And after a deep breath said, "I'm sorry about your mother. You can always board Emmett here."

Giving up, I borderline yell, "I just can't handle this anymore. I can't actually handle any more."

She listened to me cry. The oversized women in undersized shorts in the office next to mine probably did too. I got off the phone. I searched the Internet for diabetic cat chat rooms. This will be my life, I thought. I will die single. I will take care of my sick mother and sick cat. And at the end of it I will be alone.

I didn't sleep a wink that night. I call the vet on the way to work the next day, as I navigated the excruciating traffic of the 101.

"I'm going to pick Emmett up after I get off. Will you be there to show me how to use the insulin?"

The vet started to tell me something she was clearly uncomfortable saying, "Hilary. The other doctor and I were talking and we think you should leave Emmett here a while."

My guard is back up as I respond, "I don't know if I can afford that. I should probably come get him."

The vet held her position, "You mentioned putting him to sleep and we want you to know that this is not an acceptable action at this point. I would take him home myself if I had the room."

I held my ground as well, "I don't want to put him to sleep, I just don't want to put him through all of this if he isn't going to get better."

Then with an air of a person most definitely in a better position in their life than me, the vet said, "We think you need to take care of yourself at this point and get better."

I started to realize that they were not going to let me have Emmett. They were holding him hostage. This was about me.

The vet used everything she had, "Don't worry about the cat. Just worry about your mother."

Feeling judged, I said, "You aren't going to let me have my cat."

She continued what sounded like a scripted speech, "We just think you are not emotionally stable enough to take care of a sick pet right now. It will be free of charge."

I have had judgment passed on me at many points in my life. But never has a vet passed judgment on my mental state. I agreed to leave him. My mom's chemo was grueling, but I knew she was tough. She almost never complained about pain. Emmett was tough too. He almost never complained about the pain either.

Rather than negotiate with the kidnappers, I took advantage of the time. I cleaned my apartment from head to toe. I hired a carpet cleaner, Ricardo. When Ricardo came, I didn't want to look him in the eye. I knew there was cat pee everywhere. I knew the carpet was ruined and that I wouldn't get my deposit back.

Ten days later I picked Emmett up and learned about the new insulin. I thought I didn't have any more tears but they flowed freely as the vet taught me how to give the injections. The vet gave me sad eyes. I told her I was going to have to meet a guy to date in the diabetic cat chat room. I got sadder eyes.

The vet was still wary of me. She told me how much everyone loved Emmett. She made me feel guilty. But I knew there was nobody who loved him more than me. Who needed him more than me? How was I going to get through my mom's cancer without him? You know why people really find mates, because they want a witness to their life. Emmett was the witness to my life. Not something I'm proud of, but true. Kyle used to call him the Financier and sometimes when I am really sad I call him that too.

With a box of syringes on the passenger seat, I bawled all the way home and told the Financier everything was going to be okay even if it wasn't.

———————

* *My mom is doing great. She is almost officially in remission and still wearing a size small.*

GARY, MY CRAZY-ASS
HORNY MAILMAN

Luckily, my first real Hollywood writing job paid off. *My Name is Earl* was a success and lasted for four seasons. Four years of employment might not seem great to someone in a more stable business, but in the entertainment industry four years was a career. It put me in a solid financial situation at twenty-nine that intimidated most single men and I decided to buy a house. This did not help with the intimidation factor. Right after I moved in I brought a guy home after a first date. The date had gone really well. Drinks led to a famous L.A. taco stand, which led to a driving tour of L.A. At one point we found a brand-new abandoned skateboard in the middle of the road, which he took as a sign. A sign of what I didn't know. When he dropped me off, I invited him in. My house is a 1923 Spanish-style two-bedroom, two-litter-box house, in the heart of Hollywood. *Real* Hollywood meaning there are more homeless people and muggings than starlets being discovered. It's nice but not Beverly Hills. And my house is not a palace, it's about thirteen hundred square feet.

But he took one look at the living room and said, defeated, "This is the size of my entire apartment."

I never saw him again.

Around the same time as my defeated suitor left to find a

girl with a two hundred square foot apartment, I met my mail-man, Gary. He was a very friendly older mailman and seemed nice enough. But then I noticed something strange. Gary started drop-ping my mail off very very late. He'd deliver the mail sometimes as late as seven-thirty. Right after I got home from my job. He'd knock or just make loud noises so I'd come outside to chat. Then one night at eight, there was a loud series of knocks on the door. I opened it to find Gary, who is about seventy years old. Seriously.

I was surprised. "Oh, Gary. Hi."

Gary firmly said, "Hello, Hilary. (Pause.) So, you have a boy-friend?"

Instantly I got nervous, I thought for sure that he'd seen a strange guy lurking around my place. That he was making sure that it was my boyfriend and not some creep.

Upset, I said, "No. Why?"

He put his arm up and leaned into the door frame. "So, you like baseball?"

Since he could easily be my grandfather, it took me longer than usual to realize where this was going, "Yeah, I don't know much about it. But I guess I like it."

He leaned in closer and dropped his voice, "How about you, me, tomorrow night, Dodgers game?"

I was in shock. The kind First Aid books don't cover. "I—uh—well, um. My work schedule is pretty unpredictable so I can't really commit to any plans."

Instantly I realized he could tell when I was home because he could see my car in the driveway.

The panicked look on my face caused Gary to back off quickly, "Oh. Okay. Well, I thought I'd check since it didn't seem like you had a boyfriend."

This scared me. He knew a lot about me being my mailman, and certainly knew I lived by myself. A couple of weeks went by and nothing. Then one night there was knock on the door, late again. It was, surprise—Gary.

More prepared this time, I said, "I'm a little busy right now, Gary."

Gary had a prepared speech. "You like reggae, right?"

Annoyed I said, "What?"

Gary continued, "I've got tickets to the Hollywood Bowl. Reggae show. It's gonna be great."

In the most non-sexual, professional tone I could muster, I told him that I was actually dating someone now so it wouldn't be appropriate. Taken off guard, he said I could bring him. I briefly entertained asking the guy I'd been on a few dates with to come with Gary and me to the reggae show. Maybe he could bring his mailman too. But I decided this would send the wrong message. We needed professional boundaries. I wanted to be nice but this had gone too far. I politely declined.

In the days, weeks, and months after asking me out, Gary started to get progressively angrier. I seemed to be the target of that anger. I got yelled at for various things: like not having anywhere to put mail when it rains. And why do I have so many large packages? Could I get him tickets to the Oscars? Don't I work in Hollywood? One time he was confused about an express letter I wanted held for me when I was on vacation, which prompted an emotion I had never seen in my mailman before: rage. This led him to rip out several bushes along my front walkway. I never imagined I would have to tip toe around my mailman's feelings but that's what it has come to. If I had to label our relationship on Facebook I would say, "It's complicated."

Gary has lots of opinions about my mail and my life and my yard. And sometimes my mail is opened and my magazines read. I'm not going to lie, it's hard living in fear of your horny, retaliatory mailman, who now dyes his white hair jet black, but I guess it's nice to know there's one man out there who isn't intimidated by me owning my own house. So, at least I have options.

YOU DON'T BELIEVE IN LOVE

A small group of my friends decided to have a birthday dinner at a trendy Hollywood restaurant, Memphis, for my beautiful and much-skinnier-than-me friend, Kara. The restaurant looked like an old Southern mansion, complete with country fried chicken, okra, and a valet (a mixed message). It was mostly girls in attendance and one guy, who was just trying to bed the birthday girl. I was having fun. We were eating food that was bad for us and drinking more than the waitress and we knew we should. We snuck off to have slim menthol cigarettes on the porch. It was a perfect night. And there was a special attraction: a tarot card reader. What a perfect surprise.

We drew numbers to decide the order we'd go in to get our fortunes read. A new girl to the group went first. She had recently met her boyfriend and wanted to know all about him and their future together. She was gone for quite a while.

The new girl came back, thrilled. "The psychic says I'm going to marry my boyfriend!"

Everyone squealed. It seemed she and her new boyfriend were going to get married and have lots of babies. The next girl went and came back with a similar story. Exciting love connections were on the horizon, and even career opportunities. The birthday girl was told she was about to enter the best career year of her life. Everyone was praising our friend who hired the psychic. "Brilliant!" "The best idea ever!"

"Can we get her for our Christmas party?!" I was next in line, which was good, because I could hardly wait. I went to a corner of the dark burgundy bar filled with aspiring producers having meetings with aspiring actors and took a seat. She greeted me. She was younger and prettier than I thought she would be. Weren't they supposed to have warts on their noses, or is that witches? Oh, and she was French.

The psychic began. "What do you want to know?"

I didn't hesitate. "Will I ever get married?"

She spread the tarot cards neatly in front of her on the table that's wobbling had been adjusted with a stack of Splenda packets. She then turned over the kicker. The card had a picture of a guy in a black cloak holding a giant dagger. Now to the layman, this might look terrible, but I thought that bad images might actually be good in the tarot world. Things aren't exactly what they seem, right?

The psychic made some barely audible noises, and then said, "Hmm. That's not good."

I don't know much about being a psychic but one does expect a certain bedside manner. It's like when you try on a dress in Europe and they say, "It is too . . . how do you say tight in the stomach." Yeah, that's how you say it . . .

The psychic swept up all the cards. She was going to do it again. This time she told me that I had to think about "not the recent future" but more about the "future future." I should focus on love in the next year or so. I concentrated to the best of my ability; we were in a loud, popular bar. She flipped the cards over, and once again the final card showed a guy in a black cloak (popular dude in the Tarot world) in front of a church in a rainstorm being chased by dogs or something like that. (Don't hold me to what these cards exactly looked like. Whatever they were, they were bad.) The psychic's face squished up like I just shit on the table. She began to make noises like old men do where they are trying to cough something up. She then turned from her inner thoughts to me. She demanded to know if I was focusing on love in the coming year. I was a bit scared at this point. I felt like I was in third grade again and being yelled at by Miss Runte for not making plump loops on my "s." I promised her I would focus.

Trying desperately to focus, I said, "Yes, I promise. I swear on my mother's cancer. Did I mention my mother has cancer?"

No luck. She kept taking big deep sighs and rubbing her temples. I was giving her a headache. She picked all the cards up, shuffled them once again, and then gathered herself.

"Okay, I have a plan. Just focus on love in the whole span of your life. Not now or in the next year but just ever."

Now I was really nervous. Already, I'd sweated through my cute green dress. This had turned from a light fun party to a labor camp. I swear to God it looked like she crossed herself and then dealt the tarot cards again. As she turned over the last card we both held our breath. The card was . . . a guy stabbing himself in the eyes with sticks. Or at least that's what it looked like to me, but I'm not a professional. She slammed her hands down on the table.

The psychic yelled loud enough for others in the bar to turn and look, "Hilary! Hilary! Hilary!"

She leaned on her forehead and then shook her head back and forth. "What happened to you?"

I had no idea what she was talking about. "When?"

I shrugged. She was furious. "You don't believe in love!"

I'm taken aback. "What?"

The psychic continued. "You don't believe in love? How could you not believe in love?"

I tried to defuse her anger. "Is there anything about my career in there?"

175

But the psychic had laser focus. "Why don't you believe in love?"

As I looked around for my friends, for help of some kind, I said something like, "I thought I did. How do you believe in it? It exists, I know. I've seen movies about it."

I didn't know what to say. Was I supposed to tell her that I had my heart broken, not even into pieces but mashed to a pulp? That my first love slept with my best friend in his backyard trailer? That on some level, I believe I am profoundly unlovable? I didn't know what to say. She wanted me out of her sight.

I crumpled, "I'm sorry."

She said no, she was sorry. She asked for a minute before I sent the next person. She told me I needed to believe in love before anyone could help me. She gave me an audiotape of our session and asked if she could add me to her mailing list. I wanted to cry, not be added to her mailing list.

Why couldn't she have just lied? "A guy stabbing himself in the eyes with sticks is a good thing. It means you are going to fuck a twenty-three-year-old waiter and win the lottery." I was so depressed. I couldn't tell the room full of eager girls what just happened. I walked in and told them I was going to have a bunch of kids and then sadly ate a piece of cornbread or four. It was raining outside when we left and there was a cloaked man who took my valet ticket, like he knew.

SINGLE PEOPLE ARE NOT WELCOME AT BUILD-A-BEAR

I'd never been into a Build-A-Bear store, but one day while shopping at the Westside Pavilion (a mall built when real estate developers thought people hated the sun) I saw one. I went inside because I saw a stuffed cat in the window. This non-bear element intrigued me and I wondered how much that kitty in the window was. Turned out it was fifteen dollars. I picked out my orange tabby cat skin and then waited in line for the official "fluffer." While I stood there, I recorded a special audio message on a chip that they sew into the animal of your choice. I recorded it as softly as I could, but many, too many, people heard me. It was a quote from a funny cat-based humor website.

"I made you a cookie, but I eated it."

The line took forever and I kept getting looks from the staff. A cute little girl dressed like a princess came at me hard with the question on everyone's mind.

"Who is your bear for?"

"Me."

The girl and her mom looked at me with sad eyes, then immediately looked away. *Oh, please,* I thought. I've seen looks those before and it's a cat, dumb ass. Several staff members asked me follow-up questions. I can only imagine they're on guard against single people in a store filled with children, but I stuck to my guns. I told them it was for me, as an early Christmas present.

I finally got to the front of the stuffing line, where I choose a gingham fabric heart to have sewn inside its chest.

The Build-A-Bear guy looked at me and said in a sing-songy sweet voice, "Okay, now what you need to do is take that heart and rub it against your own heart and then think about all the good things and hopes and wishes—wait, is this for you?"

I nodded. I waited for him to pull some sort of emergency lever.

But instead, he just changed back to his normal much less squeaky voice, "Fine, just kiss it and give it to me."

I kissed it. I felt a little screwed that I didn't get the *whole* speech.

He fluffed it and asked, "Are you giving it to someone?"

I just shook my head no. At that point they usually allow you to press the fluff pedal yourself, or I'd heard in line from the other kids. I was not given that option. Lazy bastard.

He kept going, "Are you here by yourself?"

I nodded. He felt sorry for me. He handed me my stuffed cat and told me where I could find the accessories. I bought a Christmas tree outfit. (Which also fits my real kitty, yes, I've tried it on him a few times. Maybe taken a picture or two.) A robe, Hello Kitty panties, and bunny slippers. I paid after answering all the same questions (maybe the panties entered me into a whole new category) and left. I thought the whole thing was kind of funny until I told my friends at work and then realized it was sad. Because the truth was, I'd gone comfortably single.

PAST LIFE REGRESSION THERAPY

Every time I go to New York I visit a psychic in the West Village to have my tarot cards read. Each time I've gone, I've been with friends and the readings were shockingly accurate. When I started going it seemed fun, but now that I'm an older workaholic with nervous ovaries and a lot of questions about my future it is less fun. So the last time I went, it felt more like a gynecologist appointment. I dragged my friend Ellie through the rain and the slick cobblestones of the West Village, with only my borrowed hotel umbrella to protect us, to Esmeralda.

Our greeting when we arrived was less of a greeting and more of a stern request for me to leave my umbrella in the umbrella stand and head upstairs. Upstairs was a lounge area with a round table for readings. I took a seat at the table and shuffled her stack of tarot cards and separated them into three stacks. The psychic asked me to choose which stack I wanted read. I chose the smallest stack and she laid them out. She began by saying I'm honest to a fault. I don't like to talk behind peoples' backs. I only have a few real confidants in my life and I'm not comfortable opening up to people. This was all correct and generic. She told me I was planning an exotic vacation for the spring. This was also correct. She told me the next couple I know who gets married isn't going to make it. Then she got to the more interesting stuff.

My career is going to take off. I'll change jobs. I'll earn more money. I'll have all the success I've been working towards. She tells me all I do is work and that I've focused all my energy into that, which is true. She covered all the major areas of my life and I felt like it was building to the moment where she told me about "the one." How I was going to meet him? Where I was going to meet him? But she said nothing. Now, if you don't believe in psychics and think they are scammers then she should have noticed I didn't have a wedding ring and proceeded to tell me exactly what she knew I probably wanted to hear but she didn't.

She sighed and said, "There is no romance in the cards."

I asked her why and she told me I was completely blocked. She asked me if I knew what karma was. I should have asked her if she knew the psychic who told me I didn't believe in love! I gave her the most basic definition of karma; "If you do something bad it comes back around." She said yes, but the bad I did was not in this life. I laughed. She didn't. She told me there was not one card that represented anything about love other than past relationships. She told me that I like to date guys I can control and never actually fall for. This is exactly my problem, and had been the topic of conversation only hours before with my friend who was witnessing the reading. She gasped. The psychic told me I had to resolve my past life issues or I could never move on and be truly happy. She went on to tell the story of a woman who was having problems choking. She got to the point where she couldn't eat food anymore because she'd choke. The doctors couldn't find anything wrong with her medically so she went searching for alternative treatments and found a regression therapist. In a past life she'd been a little girl who drowned and once she tapped into that life while she was hypnotized she stopped having any problems. Now this was a lot for me to take. All I really wanted was for a woman to tell me love was around the corner, but I got more than I bargained for. She made me promise I would go into regression therapy and unblock myself. There was no other way. I promised.

Once I was back in Los Angeles, it took me twenty minutes and an Internet connection to find a past life regression therapist in my neighborhood, Hollywood, who is literally within walking distance. I found Peter Grace. He was trained by one of the pioneers of the field. His site is filled with compelling case studies. But as someone who doesn't even believe in God and lacks faith, it's a little overwhelming. Could I really be a former Samurai warrior like the newsletter describes? Do I overeat because I died in a concentration camp? Do I procrastinate because my mom had a C-section? All things the therapist has uncovered in other patients. True life stories. I don't know what's going to happen but I know it's going to happen for four hours and cost me four hundred dollars but I did make a promise to Esmeralda, who still has my hotel umbrella.

I don't know what I expected the past life regression therapist's office to look like but I did not expect it to be in a shitty '70s-style condo complex overlooking a hair salon and a BBQ restaurant. The inside was tastefully done in what looked like Pottery Barn and Mom. Peter was much younger than I thought he'd be. He mentions this right away.

"I look much younger than I am. Don't worry, I have lots of experience. Please take off your shoes."

I take off my Ugg loafers, wish I had gotten a pedicure and wonder if he was also a past life regression therapist in a past life. He directs me to what was meant to be a breakfast nook and is now a therapy nook. There's a recliner, a blanket, and a basket of pillows. I'm allowed to pick what makes me comfortable. Leaving would be the most comfortable thing at this point. I choose a wheat-filled pillow for lumbar support and put the recliner up. Peter dims the lights and I think that I should have let a friend or family member know where I was going.

The therapist starts with a questionnaire. It seems like cheating to me, because the psychic wasn't allowed to ask me a bunch of questions first. Peter asks me what my fears are (math, spiders, never getting married, never really wanting a baby). He asks me what my biggest day-to-day problem is. I tell him it is never having enough time. This time management issue comes up a few times in the hour-and-a-half long quiz. He asks me all about my parents, my sister, my childhood, how I deal with pain, anger, sadness, joy. He asks me how my parents deal with pain, anger, sadness, and joy. He asks about their health problems. Apparently, my mom's cancer was her fault. I can't wait to tell her. We discussed my health problems. Low blood sugar is most certainly related to a past life. I hope in one of my lives I was really, really skinny. I tell him I take anti-depressants, which leads him on a thirty-minute detour. He tells me sadness is a part of finding out who you are. I tell him that getting out of bed is also a part of finding out who you are. We agree to disagree.

He asks me if I ever get numbness in an arm or leg. I tell him I do sometimes when I'm asleep. He says this is a past life coming through. Our past lives come through our limbs. *Okay.* He said that people have past lives where they were shot in the Civil War and they end up having leg pain in their current life. I think about what my friend Raina said to me when I told her I was going to past life regression therapy.

"Good luck, I hope you weren't Hitler."

Luckily, I don't think I was or I would have gotten better grades in German.

MY REBIRTH

Because my mom had a C-section the first thing Peter had to focus on was my rebirth. Yes, my rebirth. It's a huge reason why I have time management problems apparently. I'm going to use that excuse on my bosses the next time I need another day on a script.

The process of rebirthing will take several hours and I'll be transported back into the womb so I can be birthed the natural way. In my mother's case, the natural way would have probably killed both of us. This doesn't seem to affect Peter's opinion. He believes C-sections are what cause a lot of our problems. We have post-traumatic stress from it. Wow, America is fucked.

If you can believe it, this was not my first rebirthing. I also had a rebirth done by two Indian women in the Maldives, who rubbed my boobs, chanted, gave me a bath, and made me sit on a box over burning incense to allow the smoke go up my vagina.

The therapist turns out the lights. I'm encouraged to get into fetal position on the floor. I decide to stay in the chair. Peter mentions I'm also allowed to use props if I feel moved to. All of a sudden I'm nervous, I didn't realize I was the one performing here. I feel like an agnostic at a Baptist Revival. I hope he didn't expect me to speak in tongues.

The therapist begins with a tone that would be condescending out of context, "Okay, let's go back. Go to your first memory."

It's vaguely of our backyard in Sherman Oaks, California, before we moved to Texas.

"Now let's go back further than you ever have before. Let's go back to before you were born. You are a fetus in your mother's womb. What is happening around you? What do you hear?"

I'm scared. I feel like I've been called to the board in Mrs. Thompson's algebra class and I don't know what I'm doing and then all of a sudden I hear my "mom's thoughts" enter my head. No shit. I'm *hearing* a conversation she's having with her OB. In slow stilted language in what sounds like my morning voice, I recount word-for-word the conversation I'm hearing. My mom's telling the doctor that she used to design swimwear and is taking time off to have kids. It seems as though she wants him to know she is smart and not just a mom. It's bizarre. I say these things out loud in this dark alcove above a BBQ place and I don't know where they're coming from.

The therapist analyzes the things I say, the things I "hear" my mom say. He then fast-forwards me to the day I was born. I recount things I know but I'm also seeing them in my head. I know my parents took Laurel Canyon from the Valley into the heart of Los Angeles to get to Cedars-Sinai Hospital. My mom is nervous but she also seems excited to see the doctor. She loves the doctor. It feels like a teacher relationship, she wants to impress the teacher. I guess I was the apple. I have no idea if this is how my mother felt at all. This is just me, in my head, in fetal position on a reclining leather chair.

At the hospital, there are problems. My dad is in the waiting room. My mother is rushed into surgery for the C-section. She is awake but out of it. She doesn't want my father in there. I'm pulled out violently.

I hear the doctor say to a nurse, "Don't tell the father."

The therapist has a field day with this one. But I didn't see what he was talking about. I have no idea what it means and at this point I don't know if I'm in a hypnotized state seeing a real past life or just having a waking dream.

The therapist talks to me about the moment I entered the world. Did I feel safe? I said "no." He has lots of opinions, and isn't shy about asserting them. He says my parents were fearful and that I was not a blessing. I wasn't the boy my dad wanted. And I was the thing that was going to keep my mother out of the real world for even longer. Then he asks me what kind of parents I wished I'd been birthed to. Not that I wanted different parents but if I could control the feelings I had that moment I entered the world, what would I choose. He asks me to think of real people I want to be birthed to. For a second I think about my friend Liam and then I realize I could never look at him again knowing I had birthed myself to him.

I say, "Can I birth myself to two caring people who just want to love me for who I am and don't have any expectations of who I am going to be or what I am going to do or not do for them?"

He lets me have this. And then it begins. I'm in the womb of a mother who is pure love. She has long flowing sun-kissed brown hair. It's parted in the middle. It *is* 1976. She's so excited to meet me. The father is equally as excited and loving with a beard. They're two people who can't hug or love enough. I come out of her vagina and into the world, it's far less traumatic, we are in their home not an operating room. There is no violent pulling. There are no nurses and drips and anesthesia. My father cuts the cord and my mother holds me. My father cradles her as she cradles me. We are a family. We are perfect just as we are. I was not born for any other reason than that they wanted to make a baby. I recite every stupid detail including the one about me coming out of the vagina to the therapist. And I have to tell you I have never felt less stupid. In fact I have never felt better. I felt like I'd had a four-hour massage on the beach in Hawaii. I felt like I'd been cuddled by a thousand puppies and kittens. I felt like I was really accepted unconditionally, something that I never really felt growing up. I pulled my lumbar pillow close to my chest and tears filled my eyes.

"Congratulations, that's how this life should have begun."

Maybe there is something to this.

PAST LIFE #1: TURN OF THE CENTURY NEW ENGLAND

I was anxious for my next appointment to get beyond rebirth and into my real past lives. I wanted to get to the bottom of my love blockage. When I tell the therapist about the psychic in New York, who sent me his way, he laughs at me.

"Psychics are charlatans."

I feel like those who live in glass condos shouldn't throw stones but then again I'm happy he's sure of what he's doing. I relax into the reclining chair where I gave birth to myself last week and get ready. We're both excited. But I panic for a minute. What if I don't see anything? He talks me through letting everything go. Letting my thoughts go. Letting my thoughts drift into blackness. Into emptiness so they can be filled by memories beyond those of this life. For what seems like five minutes it's just blackness. He says something will come. I ask which life will come.

"The life that needs to come will bubble to the surface."

I wait for bubbling. I wait for anything. My mind is an infinite field of nothing. Nothing. Nothing. Nothing. Nothing. Nothing. Nothing. Nothing. Nothing. Oh no, what if I toot? Nothing. Nothing. Nothing. Nothing. And then like a scene from *Quantum Leap* I pop into a body, into colors, into a scene, into a party. I'm a little girl in a lacy high-necked nightgown. It seems as though we are in New England at the turn of the century, there's a boisterous affair going on, with lots of guests, wine, and tables of food. I'm with another friend and it's clear from the way we're acting that we're not supposed to be awake. We keep running and hiding behind doors to take a peek at what the adults are doing. It's my friend's house and I'm her guest. We're about to run back up to bed when I see my "father." Who doesn't resemble my real father at all. I'm clearly a daddy's girl, I'm thrilled to see him. He doesn't see me. He follows a beautiful young woman into a side room and we follow too. I'm laughing and smiling and thinking we're playing a great trick on him. But then the trick is played on me when he kisses the woman, who is not my mother. I'm paralyzed. My friend says everyone knows how he is. I hit her in the arm and run back to her room. We slip into bed and my life feels like it's over.

The therapist asks me why I didn't confront him. I tell him that I couldn't, that it wasn't my place. The therapist fast-forwards me to the next morning. I'm at breakfast and my "dad" comes in full of life, he wants to fly a kite with me. But something has died in me. A trust. A love. I don't want anything to do with him. I decide right then and there I will punish him. He will never have my love again.

Peter speeds up this life until we get to the end of it. I'm alone. Never married. In a cold room. In a cold bed. He has me stay through the last breaths as my organs start to shut down and my soul drifts out of me.

"You are dead. What do you feel?"

"Relief."

It's powerful. It feels like I've uncovered a deep secret but it is secret about a life I don't remember living. It hits me this point that maybe this is just role-playing maybe your mind is given creative license to work your problems out. But the therapist is sure I really had this life and just like my rebirth he has me go back to the moment and relive it. He takes me back to the moment I saw my "father" kiss the other woman and confront him. It's hard and painful and the words come out of my mouth like stones and drop to the floor in the scene and in my therapy nook. I'm confronting my "father" in my imagination but speaking out loud, in front of another human. I'm accusing him of cheating on "my mother." I feel crazy and saner than I ever have. I don't trust men. I don't think they have good intentions. I don't think they are faithful. I have always wondered where this came from. It makes sense. This process makes sense and that scares me. What if I *was* Hitler?

PAST LIFE #2: PRE-WWII GERMAN

After dying alone to punish my unfaithful father, I thought we'd call it a day but we weren't done. I had some water and Peter began to take me down to the calm place again to the place of nothingness. I knew for sure that my brain was overworked and that this endeavor would be unfruitful. I didn't even really believe this stuff. Then all of a sudden I am on a train platform in Berlin, Germany. I worry for a second but then realize I'm in a dress. Maybe I'm Eva, but I don't think so. It's the thirties. I thought my brain was overworked but it seemed to only be warming up. I could almost smell the train station. Feel the steam. I could see the details of the flowers people held. Yellow daisies. I could see the giant train board and it's white letters and numbers flip around, changing as trains arrived and departed. I could hear the brakes on the trains and feel the cold chill in the air. I was waiting for someone.

Peter asks me if I'm excited, if I'm looking forward to the arrival of this person. I say that I'm nervous. Nervous to see this man, and then the entire story of this life starts to pour out. I'm twenty-six, an old maid at that time. My "parents" set me up with a man, whom I was supposed to marry. He left me right before we got married but now he's coming back. He said he changed his mind. I didn't want to marry him. I didn't want a man who didn't want me. But my "parents" are making me. They say I will die alone. They say I will be childless. They say he is my last chance. I wish I were waiting for anyone else. I'm jealous of the people looking forward to the train coming. Looking forward to reuniting with their husbands, wives, mothers, fathers, and lovers. The hugs have almost begun but I hope the train never comes.

We continue on in this life. A sad life. I marry this man, who cheats on me. A man who never really loves me. I have two children. I love them but I am profoundly unhappy. I have a small apartment that's impeccably clean. My children look perfect but they can never really get my attention. It was this very life I was scared of on that train platform that day. Everything I feared would come true did.

Peter wants me to fast-forward to the end. I do, but I don't get that far. I am alone. I take a bottle of pills. I let the life leave me. I think of my "children" and know my "parents" will take care of them. I think they're better off without the weight of my sadness. I drift off into a sleep I have always wanted but never had. Just as my life starts to leave me the nanny comes in with my "daughter." She sees the pills and pulls the girl away. I hear her yelling and it's over.

I was so caught up in the memories or dream or whatever it was, I forgot where I was. I forgot why I was curled up in a strange condo. It's disorienting and I'm sad. Sad for this woman, who might have been me. It's another life of disappointment. Another life where I couldn't trust men. I wonder out loud why these things are coming to the surface.

"This is your real baggage."

Our second four-hour session is up. I stumble around, put my shoes on, and write a check. I feel like I've been in an accident. I feel like I don't know who I am. I walk outside and it's now dark. It's a short but long walk to the car. I think about the new old baggage. It takes a few days and a dinner party with slightly alarmed but interested strangers for me to come to the realization that I have enough baggage in this life that I don't need to take on the baggage of my past lives, if that's what I experienced. I decide not to go back. I decide no matter how much I sometimes don't want to, that I was going to try to focus on this life. On making this life better because I would hate to still be working out these problems in a hundred years.

eREJECTION: MY FORAY
INTO ONLINE DATING

Post-many dating failures, I decided I needed to be more selective. Where can you be the most selective (choosing height, weight, religion, pet preferences) and even try before you buy? Online. Just pick one and put him in your online shopping cart. Sounded easy enough. In fact, I know many people who have had great success, like marriage success. But my experience got off to a rocky start. One dude, who viewed my online dating profile, had a singular picture of himself in a striped cardigan standing in front of a staircase and his profile started with, "I love art, architecture, exploring Silverlake, and sodomy." At least he was honest. Another person I was matched up with, Bob, listed under his occupation, "Beer. Sex. Pizza." Under his interests, "Beer. Sex. Pizza." Under who had been the greatest influence in his life, "Beer. Sex. Pizza." I don't know, maybe I'm too picky.

Online dating hasn't really worked for me yet, but I have met a lot of guys/douches/characters.

INTERNET DUDE #1: VANILLA ICE BACK-UP SINGER
Wrong Guy #1001 showed up at the Farmer's Market in a Kangol/ Newsies style cap sideways, an unbuttoned shirt with a tank top under it, shorts, and unlaced sneakers. This look was completed with

a pair of Oakleys. He got his start as a back-up singer for Vanilla Ice. I did not and I was wearing a sundress.

When he called to set the date he said, "Choose the place wisely because we could fall in love and it will have been the location of our first date." Red flag. I mentioned I was about to go to Paris with my sister and he said, "I wish I'd met you a few months earlier so we could have gone together." Red flag. I had already said yes so I felt bad backing out.

As soon as we sat down for dinner at our adorably romantic candle lit table, I knew it was doomed. He didn't seem to feel this way. Before our water even came he grabbed my hand.

"One, two, three, four. I declare a thumb war."

Red flag. We proceeded to play until he asked if it was making me uncomfortable and I said yes. He released my wet hands and we went back to dry conversation where I tried to reveal as little of myself as possible. If could have bought a blanket and covered myself up I would have. I mention Hawaii and he says, "When we go to Hawaii . . ." I mention my parents and he says, "Well, when I meet your parents . . ." I mention my sister's wedding and he says, "I'm not saying we're going to get married but if we do . . ." One, two, three, four. I declare this date is over.

INTERNET DUDE #2: VROOM. VROOM.

Andrew, early thirties, comic book artist, three dates. Posted a picture of him and his mom on his Harley motorcycle on the profile. He was a nerd, who at the age of thirty-one had finally become attractive to women and was loving it. He was trying to cultivate sex and mystery the way a thirteen-year-old boy who'd just become attractive would, hence the motorcycle. It was the same as getting a rad BMX bike. He talked in riddles and answered questions with questions.

I'm guessing he had a smoking jacket at home. He alluded to "bad boyness" but told stories about spending time with his special needs cousin and wanting to buy a house close to his family. He was awkward and confident at the same time. He kissed me in my Jetta with both of our seatbelts on, it was bizarre and then he rated me.

"Am I crazy or was that bad?"

Andrew dumped me with a pre-written dating site message, "Sorry, I have met someone else. Good luck in your search." I wish I could have responded with a message of my own, "Definitely no need to be sorry. Good luck to that someone else."

INTERNET DUDE #3: NAKED PICTURES ARE A BAD IDEA

Bennett, late thirties, small business owner. He spent too much time by himself, and I spent too much time with him. We were a neurotic mess. He told me he loved me in midst of me trying to break up with him. I responded with: "Why are you telling me that now?" He didn't have a good answer. I said it was manipulative but it kept me from breaking up with him even though I knew it was right. I did not tell him I loved him. We sat across from each other at a dark chain restaurant eating things dipped in ranch dressing. He paid with coupons. We didn't talk about the whole "I love you" thing ever. I didn't say it back, he didn't say it again. A few weeks later, we were in bed at my place and Emmett sat on my chest demanding attention, ignoring the fact that there was another male in my bed. I pet him. I admired how handsome he was.

"You are so handsome. You are such a handsome boy. I love you sooooo much. Do you know that? I love, love, love, love, love you. I love you so much."

I caught myself just as my boyfriend's cold stare caught me also. I continued to pet Emmett silently, until our respective sleeping pills took effect and the potential of a fight was over. We broke up a few days later. I learned a lot in that relationship especially that you shouldn't let anyone take naked pictures of you in a hotel bathroom that was decorated to look like a cave, even if you did feel very fit. And definitely not in a shower cap. And definitely make sure to get them back before you break up. Yikes.

INTERNET DUDE #4: THE ULTIMATE CONVERSATION

One date, one hour, one beer. The majority of the conversation was spent talking about Ultimate Frisbee. It was my date's game of choice. Lifestyle of choice. It angered him how dismissive people were of UF. It is a *sport*. A *real* sport. A difficult sport. He described the entire world of amateur and professional Ultimate Frisbee play. Yes, apparently there are professionals. He got very serious and insisted it was the most fun one could ever have. His manner however was betraying this fun. He also told me that it wasn't a Frisbee they used but a "flying disc." In my head all I could think was *who gives a flying fuck*.

INTERNET DUDE #5: THE ALMOST ONE-NIGHT STAND

Nate, early thirties, art teacher, four-ish dates. Cute. Funny. Ivy League educated. Went to camp with one of my best friends. Lives in Boston. Slept with him on the first date. Never done that before. But he was sweet and liberal and went to camp with one of my best friends! I kept expecting him to leave after. That's what movies told me about one-night stands, but he stayed. He asked to stay. I was surprised. For sure I expected him to be gone when I woke up the next morning, chewing his arm off to get out. But alas, he was not gone and he wanted to get something to eat. And even stranger he wanted to do something the next night and the next night. I'd gotten my hopes up that I'd finally had my first one-night stand, but it wasn't to be. I saw him a few more times after that and once in Boston. My only four-night stand.

INTERNET DUDE #6: SOMEONE'S EX-BOYFRIEND

Doug, mid-thirties, mid-range movie development executive, two dates. Date one, talked about how he has no use for his parents. Okay. Date two, ordered for me without asking me first at an Indian restaurant that I'd picked. Talked for quite a while about his ex-girlfriend, who I happened to know. Once he found that out I knew her he talked about her all night. I had to help him work through the break-up.

"She won't even have drinks with me!"

After that romantic dinner, he kissed me grossly on my porch open-mouth. Next day I send him a no-thank you message. The scoop from the ex-girlfriend was, "Stay away. He will smother you to death."

INTERNET DUDE #7: SPIRITUALLY COMPLETE
IN LUXURY CAR

Ian, early thirties, did something with Buddhism, one date. Long hair. Spent the whole date telling me about why he was drawn to Tibetan Buddhism and why he believes in aliens not just existing but existing on our planet right now. I'm not proud of my response, but he was cute.

"Of course we're not alone. Duh."

Drove a convertible Mercedes. Told me exactly how much money he made last year. Six figures. A few text messages the next day and never heard from him again.

INTERNET DUDE #8: "THE GYM IS MORE FUN THAN YOU"

Nick, late thirties, stand-up comedian, one date. I was his first online date. We went to a bar in my neighborhood. I ran into some friends there and he thought I had set it up on purpose, so they could check him out. His demeanor went from psychotropic drug user to psychopath.

"Well, I hope I passed your friends' little test. Please, let me know tomorrow. I'm *dying* to find out."

Totally paranoid. Totally weird. Totally left after only an hour to "hit the gym."

INTERNET DUDE #9: THE LOVE BUG

Owen, late twenties, aspiring actor/bartender. Owen, the love bug. We dated a few dates too long. He was cute. He was young. He wore smaller jeans than me. His debit card was denied at Johnny Rockets for our fifteen-dollar meal, which wouldn't have been so bad if he hadn't made a big deal out of paying since I always paid for everything.

He said as he grabbed the bill, "I do work you know."

The worst thing about your date not being able to cover a fifteen-dollar meal is his not knowing he can't cover a fifteen-dollar meal. I have always known if my checking account was below fifteen dollars even when I was fifteen. My very existence seemed to emasculate him, which was on him not me.

INTERNET DUDE #10: QUIT WHILE YOU'RE AHEAD

I dated this sweet Floridian guy for about two months but after the first few dates I already felt like I was married to him. He never left my house. I only saw his apartment once. He drove when we took my car. And I met his brother and his cousin on our third date, who he also lived with. He also didn't have much interest in having sex with me. One Sunday night he called me pretty late and wanted to come over. A perfect booty call. He came over around eleven, slipped into bed, pulled me close, and cuddled me. It was a late night booty . . . cuddle. I extracted myself and went into the living room to watch TV as a punishment—a technique I'd learned from Kyle.

Soon thereafter I called it off, over the phone. He insisted he needed to come over. I said no. He kept saying he had something for me. I said I didn't want it, but I appreciated the thought. About six months later, I got a package delivered by a messenger to my office. The card said something like, "This is what you missed out on." He'd made a small clay sculpture of me, with a creepy far-off stare, crooked nose, and fish-like eyes. Yes, I had definitely missed out on something. Thank God. What's weird is that I'd been in a similar situation before. With me, guys seem to be all in or in somebody else.

PART 6

WHERE DO BROKEN VAGINAS GO? DO THEY FIND THEIR WAY HOME?

MY BROKEN VAGINA

Comfortably single ladies, like me, love out-of-town three-day events with free booze—weddings, funerals, conferences, reunions—mistakes might be made but forgotten by the time you catch the return leg of your flight. You can pretend that the guy you hooked up with was really the love of your life but he lives in Ohio and there's just no way to make it work. I admit, I've allowed myself to engage in a few of these trysts and only one left me with a broken vagina.

As the doctor formulated that very diagnosis, my legs and chipped red toenails were up in the stirrups and there was an uncomfortable draft. The table was directly under an air vent on at full-blast, which still didn't prevent me from sweating up a nervous storm and sticking to the butcher paper the nurse had rolled out under me just like my waxer does. I could smell the powder from the latex gloves.

After far too long being in this uncomfortable position, she said, "So, I'm taking a closer look."

I'd been to that office just a month earlier seeing another doctor, a male doctor. I told him that over the course of a few days I had been to a reunion and in a car accident and now some unusual stuff was happening down there at the wrong time of the month. My accident was on the way home from the set of *My Name is*

Earl, where I still worked as a writer. It had been a long day and I'd brought Emmett to work not because I'm crazy but because the episode was about a cat show. On the way home after a fourteen-hour day, me and my 2001 Jetta were rear-ended on an exit ramp from the 101 freeway. Emmett's cage flew forward and hit the dash. My neck snapped back when my seat belt caught me. I got out of the car and yelled at the driver.

Furious in the middle of the busy freeway ramp, I yelled, "My fucking cat is in the car you asshole."

He wouldn't get out of his station wagon until I started visibly crying. He said he was sorry. He said he didn't hit me that hard. It was clear he was trying to assess if I was going to sue him and that's all he cared about. My neck was killing me.

The next day I went to the emergency room and got muscle relaxers and a neck brace and a once over by the nurse. Then a few hours later, I started bleeding. Down there. That's why I went to the doctor. He said he'd take a look, but it was probably nothing.

The male doctor, an internist, not a gyno, commented as he looked around in there, "Well, you have a very tiny uterus."

Flattered, I said, "Oh, thank you."

He told me everything looked normal. I knew in my gut that wasn't true. He asked me if I was sexually active. I said yes. I'd just hooked up with at guy at my reunion. He asked how recently, and I said, "a few nights ago."

"Well," he said, "at least you're getting some, right?"

The sexual partner I "got some" from was a guy I met at a reunion for a screenwriting internship program I did. He was the first guy I had sex with in my new house. He had olive skin, brown eyes with specks of what looked like gold foil, and had read something other than just *The Unbearable Lightness of Being* by Milan Kundera. That was enough for the frisky literary snob in me. We had the best sex of my life, mostly due to the fact that he had a partially numb penis from some sort of unexplained childhood skateboard accident. Bad for him. Good for me. It allowed him to have sex for over four hours. Upon hearing this, a girl at the office said, "If I couldn't make a guy cum after four hours I would hang up my pussy." I don't have your typical workplace.

The male doctor continued. "You said you met him at a reunion?"

Uncomfortable, I squirmed, "Yeah, at a reunion. It's like shooting fish in a barrel."

I had never used that phrase before and certainly not to a doctor who had his fingers in me. He put his free hand up as if to high-five me. I looked to the female nurse standing in the corner. She looked away as if to say she wouldn't testify. I was horrified but I also felt sorry for the doctor. I think he tries to be funny for his writer patients. He's not funny. He will never be funny.

The doctor wrapped it up with a Sex Ed speech, said I probably skipped a birth control pill, which would explain the unusual activity. I knew I didn't. I knew he was wrong. I'd been on the pill since I was seventeen and dating the surf music obsessed guy who worked at a record store. Nowadays I would forget my address before I would forget to take that pill.

A month later, I was still having problems, so that's why I was back in the stirrups. The woman doctor didn't say much of anything as she looked, just made noises and sighs, which indicated a) something was terribly wrong and b) she had poor bedside manner. Her taking "a closer look down there" meant bigger instruments and more than the usual discomfort.

The female doctor sighed and then half-under her breath said, "This looks unusual."

That's something you never want to hear from your gyno a month after you've had a one-night-ish stand. I decided that if that guy gave me an STD, I was going to take out a full-page ad in his hometown paper. "Local Man has Dirty Dick! Here's his picture and phone number."

The female doctor continued, "Um, it looks like you've torn your cervix."

She went on to explain that it was ripped and even drew me a picture of it: it looked like a pink bleeding diamond.

I was stunned. "Doctor, are you telling me that I *broke* my vagina?"

The female doctor didn't hesitate. "You could say that."

Shouldn't she have corrected me? Given me a medical term that I could tell my parents. My feet were still in stirrups, and I was covered in lube as she told me my cervical tissue could be worn thin because of cancer. Great. How was I going to tell my family that I also had cancer? How was my mom supposed to deal with that, just as her hair was starting grow back in and she was finishing up her treatment for breast cancer. I wouldn't be able to tell them that. I would have to keep it all to myself. The doctor said that I might need stitches, that it could have left me vulnerable to an STD, that there would have to be tests and specialists and silver nitrate to promote healing applied directly to the wound. *My* wound. The doctor finally left. And I was left in the room with a flickering fluorescent light. She told me to take my time, but I was late to my bikini waxer. The ball-buster Vladka.

I couldn't be late, she doesn't tolerate it. I got out of the stir-rups, pulled on my underwear with a ironic rhinestone dollar sign on them, and leaned down for my jeans when BLACK. I went completely unconscious. I woke up on the probably-not-clean-floor thinking of pancakes, staring at a poster on heart health. I thought I was dying from my broken vagina. I wondered what the coroner's report would say. I wondered if Writers' Guild Health Center would put up a little plaque where my friends could leave flowers and stuffed animals. I was so tired from everything. Tired from life. And I was on the floor of a ten-dollar co-pay clinic at my personal rock bottom. My ten pounds of extra ass, despite months of starving myself on Atkins, hung out of my front-less gown. I never wanted to move off that floor.

I closed my eyes again, but I knew they couldn't stay closed for long; my waxing appointment was in thirty minutes. And for whatever reason that gave me hope. It gave me purpose. She listened to me talk about my broken heart, my mom's cancer, the latest somebody who becomes nobody fast. She waxed me within a few hairs of nothing. Not even a butt hair spared. She made me feel sexy and womanly even when everything in my life seemed to be falling apart. She was a cold hard woman who wasn't surprised by anything because she'd seen it all. There was immense comfort in that. Nothing new here, just the human experience.

I summoned the energy to reach up and open the door to the examination room. I crawled into the hall and flagged down a nurse, my rear-end on full display for the patients awaiting lung x-rays. I barely held back my tears. I left a trail of lube on the floor like a snail. The nurse wanted to get me juice but I told her I didn't have time for juice—I needed to get to my waxer ASAP. They said legally they couldn't let me leave without drinking the juice. I tossed it back like a shot, and then got dressed. And like a Domino's pizza, in less than thirty minutes my legs were back up and I was in Vladka's office in the rear of that Vietnamese nail salon, with bright colors, bad décor, and a half a dozen women yelling. And while I told her about my broken vagina, she worked her magic down there and up there.

"It will all pass."

And she made me believe it would. [1]

---

[1] Update: Since this story was written, everything has healed properly. No cancer or weirdness and my vagina is now up and running again. I did see the unfunny doctor recently and after inspecting my pooper he said, "A+ for cleanliness." Got to love Dr. Inappropriate.

AN UN-SPIRITUAL AWAKENING
ON PARKING LEVEL 4

After finding Kyle's book and almost losing it in Barnes & Noble, I run directly to my car in the parking lot and cry my eyes out. I pound the steering wheel; I leave tear-filled messages on friends' cell phones. And then I call him. I call to leave him an angry message but I end up leaving a sad one.

I sit in my noble Jetta with my broken vagina. Life has beaten me up. Cat Diabetes. Breast Cancer. Hurricanes. Heart attacks. Losing the man I thought I was going to marry. Bad sex. Bad relationships. Guys who saw my boobies and didn't call me again. Weight issues. Feline acne. Being used and abused emotionally by others and myself. And just today being referred to as the "fat-assed girlfriend" in my ex-boyfriend's novel. I'd experienced it all and I'd been praying to the universe that I'd just get a fucking break.

Kyle calls me back and I give him a piece of my mind and then cry. He doesn't have much to say. He tries to say it's not me in the book, even though conversations are word for word. He ends up talking in circles until it becomes clear that he wasn't trying to assassinate my character or my fat ass, he was just lazy. He was too lazy to invent a backdrop for his novel, so he stole ours. The knight in shining armor marriage proposal that happened on our first date. My Groundlings classes. Our neighborhood. The night I gave him an almost hand job under the table at a bar. He tells me there are two girls in the book and I'm kind of both of them. One girl he meets represents someone at the beginning of a relationship, the way they're happy and bullshit free. They love sex and hanging out and don't expect anything yet. He tells me that used to be me. But that's an insult because it doesn't tell the whole story. I didn't change. We changed together. It takes two to not want to have sex. One to say "no" and the other to make the person *want* to say "no." He didn't make me feel like having sex. He made sex some sort of thing you check off your list. Teeth brushing. Crap. Bath. 69. Sex. Sleep.

He asks me if I am going to read the whole book. I say no, even though I don't know. He seems hurt. I want him to be hurt. I want him to think I will never read it, because he wants me to. He tells me that there's a part where the main character cums in his girlfriend's shampoo for color-treated hair bottle. He wants me to know he never actually did that. I tell him now I really know I'm never going to read the book.

Then I begin telling a story with no segue, a story about a girl and her broken vagina. I tell him all of the nitty-gritty details. Where I met the guy ("the cervix buster"). How long we had sex. That it was great. That it was the first time I had ever finished from just straight sex. I even got down to the length of the injuring object (which I made a replica of for my friends at work with a napkin, a large napkin). I finish and there's silence.

Then after he takes a deep breath, Kyle says, "That isn't a story any ex-boyfriend EVER wants to hear."

Then it's my turn, "I know, Kyle. I know."

I WIN.

FOURISH
MONTHS
LATER

THE LAST SUPPER, OLIVE GARDEN STYLE

I'm sitting at the Olive Garden across the table from the person who's hurt me more than anyone else I've ever dated, and certainly hurt me more than anyone else who has ever written a book about me. And I asked him to be here. When Kyle's book came out, I had a lot of anger. And that anger seeped out from what was clearly an unhealed wound. When Kyle broke up with me I took every greeting card and love note and small gift he'd given me (sans the one piece of jewelry he bought me after I demanded a gift that didn't come from Best Buy) and put them in a cardboard box. I didn't have enough time to mourn, I had to get an apartment and a job and figure out what the fuck I was doing with my life. So inside that box, I also put the love I had for Kyle and the hate I had for him and just moved on. It was like sewing up a deep cut without cleaning it out first. Not surprising it got infected.

What prompted our dinner together was film. I found about thirteen old rolls of film (remember those) and I didn't know when they were from. Little mysterious time capsules. I got the pictures developed at a West Hollywood Target and they were all of Kyle and me. I flipped through them in the lobby by the elevators like a person in a movie who has just solved a crime by something that appeared in one of the photos. I thumbed through all the pictures, mouth agape. The pictures were most of vacations I'd forgotten we'd even taken. Us at Waikiki Beach, during our first trip to Hawaii. At Pearl Harbor, one of the few things I ever saw move Kyle. Our first snorkel and first introduction to freaky fish. The North Shore and our first introduction to freaky surfer hitchhikers. Maine, where did they get that "e"? Martha's Vineyard, for a Lobster bake wedding. Catalina Island birthday trip complete with golf cart tour and sex in a hotel bed. All these trips we had to save up for months to go on, but they were worth it. At least for me. These photographs documented our entire relationship and all the haircuts/hair colors I had during that time. The only people who love unnatural red hair dye as much as I did in my twenties are Germans.

These tiny time capsules I'd unearthed ripped me apart. How can you have these memories? These beautiful memories and have everything go so wrong. I'd never seen myself look happier. I am not shitting you there was a goddamn twinkle in my eye on the ferry to Martha's Vineyard. How can the guy in these pictures break up with the girl in these pictures when she is at one of the lowest points in her life? How can he smile at her like this and then call her his "fat-assed" girlfriend a hundred times in his book? If I could just say, "Oh, I dated a dick," and move on, I would have already. I'd had my victory in my parking lot over Kyle, telling him about my broken vagina. Not leaving him to wonder about the details. But it was a victory in the war with him not a victory for me as a person because it was dependent on his reaction. A true personal victory isn't dependent on anything but your own response. I needed to get over Kyle for real, and not just in the way girls say they are over someone as they slam down another seabreeze.

I called Kyle. The last time I'd talked to him was in that parking lot conversation, post–finding the book trauma. I'd just broken up with another guy, who I was sure I was going to marry until among other things he started stealing toilet paper from hotel rooms. To the one guy who is reading this book, don't do that. That is way unattractive. So, I told Kyle I wanted to get together to talk about our relationship. He said okay. He still had that girlfriend he had when we went to that upscale Italian meal and he'd innocently told me he sold a book, but he told me that he wasn't going to marry her. Did she know that?

Kyle and I met at the Olive Garden in Westwood for our big dinner, where of course we'd spent so many nights before. I hadn't been back since we broke up. Neither had he. When I pulled into the parking garage, I could taste the salad and breadsticks and feel them waiting to expand the fat cells I'd worked so hard to shrink at my fancy gym. Kyle got there early and I was a little late. I walked up to the small bar seemingly in a hallway and there he was, drinking a Bud. He looked older but the same. We hugged. We waited for an eternity for a table but it was enough time for us to both get buzzed. After we were finally awarded a table for surrendering our glowing square, we ordered our regular orders and I begin something I'd rehearsed in my head. A confession.

To this man, who has hurt and betrayed me, I began to tell the truth. There was no posturing, though a little fidgeting, in the faux leather booth. This was for me. I tell Kyle I dream about him and I don't think this is normal so many years after breaking up. I tell him that I haven't been in love since we broke up. I tell him I don't know if I can. My spirit is no fool; it's learned its lesson. I'm embarrassed by what I'm hearing come out of my mouth. But it *is* the truth. It's why reading Kyle's book in the store that day hurt so much. I hadn't been honest with myself. In my head there was part of me that thought I would end up with Kyle. He destroyed that with his book. I was angry not just about him betraying our past but him betraying our possible *future*. I finish my rant/cry. I know Kyle has a girlfriend. I don't want anything from him; I just want to hear myself tell the truth. He smiles and he tells me he has thought the same things. He tells me he dreams about me all the time. He tells me he wonders if breaking up was the biggest mistake of our lives. He was worried he would never make it as a writer. That we would get married and he would lose his drive. That he would get stuck supporting me, which is funny since I made more money than him the entire length of our relationship. He thinks now that maybe he does want to get married and that he does want to have kids. He is successful now and he loves his sister's kids. He thinks that we took our connection for granted. That we thought what we had together was something we could easily find. He doesn't have that kind of relationship with his girlfriend even though there are lots of things he likes about her. He says he's thought about what it would be like if we were still together.

Our food comes. Chicken parmesan for him and salad and breadsticks with a dipping sauce (half marinara/half alfredo) for me. The UCLA students who sit around us laughing and celebrating some sort of college achievement that won't matter in the least when they graduate are unaware at the emotional torture that is going on at our table. He has my heart in a vice. This is not just a standard meal at a chain restaurant. We eat silently thinking about what has just been said. I pull out the pictures I've gotten developed. He flips through them. We help each other fill in the blanks where our own memories have failed. I cry. He tells me that there is nothing to be sad about. He's trying to comfort me but I don't know enough about what I am feeling to be comforted. I don't know if I love or hate him.

Tipsy, we head to a nearby bar in a fancier restaurant that doesn't have endless bowls of pasta, to continue whatever this is. Discussing the good times feels like crawling under the covers during a rainstorm. The bad memories seem so far away. It's intoxicating to know that there was someone who used to love me. I know this is wrong. Don't judge me. I was just looking for my Hollywood ending. What if Kyle wasn't just an asshole I dated? What if he didn't just write a mean book about me? What if he was the one? Then it would turn a hideous, embarrassing story into the greatest love story ever told. Guy writes book. Girl writes book. They come back together to write the book of love. I've seen enough Drew Barrymore movies to know that it can work like this and you have too. I ask Kyle if he's thought of kissing me since I arrived at dinner, because I just need to know that he thinks I'm pretty. It's so pathetic and I hate what I am saying. He said yes and that he hasn't just thought about it tonight. This shouldn't make me smile but it does. I'm an alcoholic sitting in front of a frosty beer at a bar where nobody I know hangs out.

We give each other drunken compliments and trade stories we've missed in each other's lives (Claire is divorced and a lesbian now—a *real* lesbian—my mom is done with chemo, my sister is getting married and I'm not invited). The bartender treats us like a couple.

Kyle and I are not a couple anymore but the idea of being one, in this moment, is for some reason as intoxicating as the vodka sodas. The book now seems like foreplay. Advanced braid-pulling foreplay. I drive Kyle to his car. We hug a long hug and then he gets out. He's scared to stay in the car any longer, scared that we might take it too far; he doesn't want to do that to his girlfriend. Sure, respect *her*. We say we'll be in touch. I go home and can't sleep.

The next day I tell my friends what happened. I'm met with horror. "Why would you go out with him?" They remind me of things I've temporarily forgotten about. Remember when Kyle called me his "fat pig girlfriend" at a party. Remember that he never told me I was beautiful. Remember when he told me I shouldn't wear skirts because I look fat in them. Ah, I remember. Remember when he left me after I lost my job. Remember how he forgot what I ordered at Olive Garden. Remember how I was never enough for him. My giddiness fades. I call him and he backtracks. We both do. I am angry. I am sad. I am mad at myself. I begin to mourn our relationship for the first time.

Shortly after our last supper at Olive Garden, the grand OG closed its doors. A chapter was over in its life and mine. I had to finally accept Kyle was not the man I am going to marry. He is not the man who I'm going to be pregnant with. He is not the man who is going to rub my belly as we lie in bed and talk about baby names. Our baby will not be named Dead or Robot. It will not have stringy blonde hair and cuss like a sailor. Maybe I won't have a baby with anyone. But I had to finally accept the truth about Kyle. He was never the one. And that's okay. He doesn't have to be the one. Our entire relationship isn't invalidated. It was meaningful just maybe not in the ways I thought it was. My relationship taught me the ultimate lesson.

One of my favorite books growing up was Shel Silverstein's *The Missing Piece*. I loved it. I read it over and over again. This Pac-Man like figure sets off, searching for his missing piece. And he can't find a piece that fits. That fills his hole. That's how I've felt all my adult life, ever since I left for college. Since I left behind my parents, my small Texas town, my Republican politics, my first boyfriend . . . I've always been looking for something to make me whole. In friends. In jobs. In men. In Kyle writing his book and me writing mine. I have found something. If this really was the Hollywood movie it would be my true love. Paul Rudd/Luke Wilson/Jason Schwartzman would be my nerdy best friend who I thought was just my friend, but really he's the one. But nothing like that has happened. I have a really good cute male friend, Len, but we slept in a twin bed in Turkey together and we were like brother and sister.

All my life I have searched high and low for something and I think I've finally found it. In *The Missing Piece*, the little guy finally finds a piece that fits but realizes the most important thing was that he was complete all along. And so was I. I was complete long before I met Kyle. Before he told me he loved me. Before I had sex for the first time in that trailer. Before I had my first kiss on that trampoline. And I might not fully know who I am yet, I might still give the occasional accidental hand job, or on a dark day roast a marshmallow over my gas cook top, but at least I'm not looking to fill anything anymore. Because the missing piece I was always looking for, was me. *I* was whom I was waiting to meet. And even though my house smells like cat pee, my friends say I'm a catch.

EPILOGUE

The whole time I've been writing this book and seemingly my entire adult life, my cat Emmett has been sick. For the past few months, he has been confined to my kitchen with a baby gate. He would stay up at night pushing on it and meowing for my attention until he lost his voice. I'm going to apologize here for the night I called him an "asshole" at four a.m.

Every morning I'd spend a half-hour cleaning up cat pee and another half-hour giving him medicine and love and denying that he was dying. Emmett has bounced back from many illnesses, so it made sense that I could make myself believe he'd bounce back from this one too. In the Spring of 2010 he was diagnosed with a pituitary gland tumor and it turned out it was the root of all of his problems: his diabetes, his heart condition, his weak legs, his thin and dandruffy skin. It was finally diagnosed when he went into heart failure and a cardiogram revealed his heart was growing. Opposite of the Grinch, it was growing two-sizes too big. Emmett's pituitary gland was secreting too much hormone because of a tumor. It was basically cat gigantism, which was ironic because Emmett had never looked smaller and sicker. He was tired and slept a lot but he was never too tired to run across the room for a "cookie." Lolly sensed he was dying and began to take care of him. She'd sleep in the kitchen at night, just watching over him. One night I accidentally stepped on his tail and she jumped at me like, *"Watch it because I can take you out and then eat your body, bitch!"* Being eaten by my pets after I die has always been a fear of mine and an actual risk when living alone with cats.

Not long ago as summer neared its end, I noticed Emmett was not doing well. One day he actual fell asleep with his head in the water bowl, which was adorably heartbreaking. The radiation had not done the trick. The cocky pet oncologist had not done the trick. In our one visit he mentioned his wife a million times. It was so obvious he didn't want to get the single cat lady's hopes up. Emmett was a trooper through all the medications and treatments, but I'm not going to lie, so was I. I have been to a lot of vets. A lot of specialists. Written big checks, when I had it and when I didn't because Emmett was a top cat.

From the day I picked Emmett out at the feline foster home in Virginia, I knew we were meant for each other. All the other kittens were happily playing with a feather teaser, when Emmett marched up, took the teaser in his mouth, and dragged it under the couch. The foster mom apologized for his behavior and I said I'd take him. His eyes were so big they barely fit on his little kitty head. Eventually, he grew into them and into a very handsome boy. Picking out his sister was easy. Lolly was quiet and beautiful. I drove them home in the same Ford Explorer I locked myself in when my high school boyfriend cheated on me that I'd gotten for my sixteenth birthday. I told the cats we didn't know each other but that we were going to get to know each other and that was going to be the fun part. We got back to my lavender bedroom at my haunted apartment (next book) and took a nap together. The three of us. My family. I was twenty-one then. I didn't know it would still be just the three of us at thirty-three. But it is. It was.

The last few nights of Emmett's life, I stayed up with him. All three of us, on the bed, just like it started. I reminded them of all the great adventures we'd had (that car trip across country where Lolly burrowed into the mattress box spring at a Red Roof Inn and my dad wanted to leave her, "We knew there would be some casualties."). I recounted old boyfriends, good and bad, that we'd also shared a bed with. I told Emmett what a good pet he'd been, and that I was so lucky to have gotten to know him. I told him, "You're the reason why I have a book but you are also probably the reason I don't have a husband. But I love you anyway."

I wanted Emmett to die at home but after a few truly restless nights, I knew it was time and I had to do what was right. It's a promise we make as pet owners that we will put them above ourselves at the end. I called the vet and had to hang up because I couldn't even talk. I finally practiced a few times and called back. I made the appointment for the next morning. One more day. One more day with my baby.

I texted Kyle. I wanted him to have to chance to say goodbye, he did parent Emmett for almost five years. I left work at lunch and met him at my house. It had been years since he'd seen Emmett. He was shocked at his skinny, sick body. But Emmett had more energy around Kyle than he'd had in weeks. He pawed at Kyle and looked up at him meowing, and that's when Kyle saw the Emmett he knew. In those big green eyes that once again were too big for his head.

Kyle and I shared memories of Emmett. He told me that right before I came home from New York, when he had decided to break up with me, he took a nap with Emmett and that it was really special. I have taken lots of naps with Emmett so I don't know what it was about this nap that meant so much to Kyle, maybe it was because it was their good-bye nap, but it made Kyle cry. And there we are in my cat hospice of a bedroom crying together. We had not really cried together since the day we moved out of our apartment. Kyle stopped loving me but he didn't stop loving Emmett. To break the tension Kyle points out my visualization board and makes fun of it, it helps remind me that even though Kyle loves animals, we are not meant for each other.

We take Emmett outside to the garden he loved, to sit in the sun and talk. We talk about how hard it is, but that it has to be done. Kyle gets unsure for a second but then apologizes. I've had the "benefit" of dealing with this for a while. Kyle was playing emotional catch up. Emmett was the last real connection between us, and he was dying in front of us literally. But I'm so glad Kyle was there, because nobody else understood who Emmett was. He was Em. He was Emmentaler. He was Emberly. He was Emmetron. He was Emmett Otter. He was the Biggest Boy in the World. He was Korfalaque. He was the Financier. He was my best friend. And to everyone but Kyle that sounds crazy.

That night I monitored Emmett's breathing, gave him spoonfuls of water, kissed him more times that I probably had in his whole life, rubbed his little ears, and bought a necklace online like the one Carrie wears on *Sex and the City* with his name on it, so he could continue to ruin my dating life from beyond the grave.

I took Emmett to the vet the next morning, in a laundry basket with a piece of his favorite plant lying next to him. When I would let him outside for supervised visits he would make a beeline for that plant and I would reprimand him that he was wasting his outdoor time but he didn't care. I stayed with Emmett during the whole procedure, holding his paw and thanking him. I promised him that I was going to be okay. That Lolly was going to be okay. And I felt the life go out of him in a very peaceful way.

The vet helped me donate his body to science, and I think that he'd like that. And I'll be proud when a young vet student opens him up and sees his giant heart that I knew was giant way before he got sick.

Emmett, you were such a good boy.

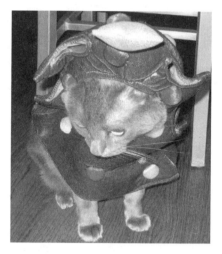

Emmett Otter Winston (1998–2010)

ACKNOWLEDGMENTS

First and foremost, I want to thank my parents for only reading this page in my book and for allowing me to pursue every intellectual/artistic whim I had as a child. From painting on the heads of nails to making a replica of Notre Dame out of balsa wood to raising ducks in our guest bathroom. Though we don't say it a lot, I love you guys. Also, thanks Mom for still making me Rice Krispies Treats on my birthday and thanks Dad for still giving me cash when you drop me off at the airport even at thirty-four.

I'd also like to thank my sister, Christine, who had a lot taken from her but wouldn't allow it to take her down. She's the strongest person I know. I would also like to thank her for NEVER unlocking the door to the bathroom we shared growing up because facing such unfairness and adversity at a young age only made *me* stronger. And if I'm handing out "I love you"s, you get one too.

I'd like to thank Glynn Owens for being the first person to call me out when I was wearing an "I don't believe the liberal media" shirt. I hope you're drinking a beer on a fluffy white cloud laughing at me since I have now become the liberal media.

Thank you to Mickey Berman at ICM, one of my agents and one of my best friends. You are the only person I talk to almost every day and you know more about me than my therapist. Sorry.

Big thanks to ICM's Andrea Barzvi, my literary agent. You and I both know where we started. I couldn't have done this without you. And thanks for saying that girl had fat ankles.

Thanks to Laura Swerdloff, my editor, for "getting me" and telling me I was going to have good karma for leaving out that one story.

Thank you to my patient feature agents at ICM, Nicole Clemens and Ava Jamshidi, who believed in this book when it was just an embryo.

Thank you to Prince and Erica, who have really been there through thick and thin. And in thin they have showed just what incredible friends they are. I wouldn't want anyone else's face on a coaster or anyone else making fun of my caveman space work. Also a special thanks to Erica for letting me talk in excess about my broken vagina with her husband (calm down, he's a doctor).

Thank you to Lee, my fake boyfriend, who takes me to fancy dinners and tells me when I look skinny. I wish we wanted to marry each other.

Thank you to the Ladies Poker Group (Missi, Christine, Brooke, Jill, Laura). You saved me, plain and simple. And you taught me more than I ever wanted to know about . . . well, you know what.

Thank you to Greg Garcia, who wrote the best pilot I have ever read and hired me to work on his show. And amazingly continued to re-hire me season after season even after finding out I was this crazy.

Thank you to the *Community* and *My Name is Earl* writing staff for listening to all these stories ad nauseum including Danielle AKA "Best Buddy," Victor, and "Bowlie," who read this at a very, very early stage during the Writer's Strike and told me it wasn't terrible.

Thank you to Professor Patricia Griffith, an awesomely talented writer, woman, teacher, and Texan. My entire career is really dedicated to her because without her nudging and encouraging I would be a very unhappy lawyer right now. And I certainly couldn't throw around words like "hand job" and "vagina" at a law firm.

Thanks to Marie, who has been listening to all my dating stories since the day we met on the roof of the Everglades dorm in the summer of '95. You are the truest of true friends.

I would like to thank Recess, The GW comedy troupe that took a chance on an awkward loner, who pronounced "nuclear" wrong and changed my entire life. Specifically, Matt AKA "Flanny," Ptolemy, Chris, and Jennie. Matt and Jennie also made this book much better, warmer, and funnier than it was going to be.

Thanks to Lauren and Justin, the East Coast Superstars to my West Coast Superstar, and the best free therapists ever.

Thank you to Soraya and Jose, for always being there and always laughing with me at things we probably should have been crying at.

Thanks to Debbie Deb Deb for always letting me share and sharing candy with me.

Thank you to Rich, Eric, and Shana. The Legality Pillow. The Onion Bunny. The trailer. Sophie B. Hawkins. The defining summer of my life.

Thanks to my best friend in middle school, Megan. I have the sense of humor I have because of you. Because of the bunny puppet videos we made and songs our band, Vegetarians with Rifles, sung.

Thank you to teachers who made a difference. Mrs. Davis (fourth grade). Mrs. Loomis (sixth grade). Mrs. Nelson (seventh grade). Mr. Parks (ninth grade). Mrs. Case (ninth grade). Mr. Reagan (tenth grade). Dr. Barnett (twelfth grade).

Thanks to Jared Levine, Alex Kohner, and Ted Gerdes for the legal eagle stuff. And a special thanks to Jared and Ted, who were some of the first men to read the book and gave me hope that they wouldn't be the last men to read it.

An ex-boyfriend once asked me if Emmett were a man would I marry him. I took way too long to answer and that was enough of an answer. Thank you to my dear sweet Emmett, who was there through it all. I love you and miss you so much but I hope you're in cat heaven where you can play with Lulu, Binker, Pierre, Tavi, and Licky. At the risk of sounding like a crazy cat lady (too late), I really couldn't have made it through anything in this book without you and Lolly, who I also love very much. Though I really wish Lolly did more around the house.

And finally, thank you to the guy I end up with, who will read this book and still want to be with me. Good luck.

226